"Imagine immersing yourself in the wisdom of body-centered awareness from thousands of years of practice under the compassionate and skilled guidance of an experienced and illuminating practitioner. *Yoga Skills for Therapists* is Amy Weintraub's gift of fresh air that weaves detailed instructions for personal and clinical applications with what modern research is now demonstrating to be effective clinical interventions for anxiety, depression, and trauma. Even your own mental and physical health will be greatly enhanced with the accessible steps illustrated in this fabulous contribution to our human journey toward well-being!"

—**Daniel J. Siegel, MD**, Executive Director, Mindsight Institute; Clinical Professor, UCLA School of Medicine; author, *The Mindful Brain, The Mindful Therapist,* and *Pocket Guide to Interpersonal Neurobiology*

"Amy Weintraub represents the new masters of yoga . . . who will carry the art and science into the new millennium. She is one of the forerunners of integrating yoga and therapeutic modalities, and I highly commend her for courageously pioneering this field where others will follow."

—**Rama Jyoti Vernon**, co-founder, *Yoga Journal*; founder, Unity in Yoga

"A psychotherapist might spend many years studying yoga and still not achieve anything near this elegant, practical, powerful integration."

—**Donna Eden & David Feinstein, PhD**, co-authors, *Energy Medicine* and *The Promise of Energy Psychology*

"Weintraub, a leader in the field of yoga therapy, offers evidence-based, easy-to-introduce strategies for managing anxiety, improving mood, and relieving suffering . . . making it easy to apply the wisdom of yoga effectively in the therapeutic context." —**Kelly McGonigal, PhD**, author, *Yoga for Pain Relief*, editor-in-chief, *International Journal of Yoga Therapy*

"I offer gratitude for Amy Weintraub's book, which provides those of us in the helping professions with a rich medley of well-designed interventions that enable us to integrate the powerful and now research-proven healing modalities of yoga into our daily interactions with clients."

—**Richard Miller, PhD**, author, *Yoga Nidra: The Meditative Heart of Yoga;* president, Integrative Restoration Institute

"While this book is written for psychotherapists, I highly recommend it to yoga teachers and practitioners looking to understand the mood-management power of yoga's deeper practices."

—**Danna Faulds**, author, *Into the Heart of Yoga* and *Go In and In*

"*Yoga Skills for Therapists* will become a timeless guide for therapists at all levels of experience."

—**Richard P. Brown, MD**, Associate Professor in Clinical Psychiatry, Columbia University College of Physicians and Surgeons; co-author, *Non-Drug Treatments for ADHD* and *The Healing Power of the Breath*

"... a concise, easy-to-read book that helps healers center themselves and, by doing so, expand the circle of healing to encompass others."

—**Shirley Telles, MBBS, PhD**, Director of Research, Patanjali Research Foundation, Haridwar, India; head, Indian Council of Medical Research Center for Advanced Research in Yoga & Neurophysiology

"... an indispensable contribution to the emerging field of integrative mental health. This exceptionally clear and comprehensive discussion of time-honored and effective body–mind interventions should be required reading for all psychotherapists."

—**Rubin Naiman, PhD**, Clinical Assistant Professor of Medicine, University of Arizona Center for Integrative Medicine; author, *Healing Nights: The Science and Spirit of Sleeping, Dreaming & Awakening*

"... well-written and well-researched ... simple, easy-to-apply but powerful breathing, meditation, and hand gesture techniques that do not require a mat or body postures. Therapists can easily incorporate these techniques into their practices without otherwise having to change what they do, and clients can use them on their own. Thank you, Amy, for giving us access to this ancient healing wisdom."

—**Richard C. Schwartz, PhD**, developer, Internal Family Systems Therapy; author, *Introduction to the Internal Family Systems Model*

"*Yoga Skills for Therapists* brilliantly opens a door to the physical and spiritual layers of a client—one that therapists and counselors have been waiting to walk through ... From a place of genuine respect, integrity, and intention, Amy offers easily applied foundational yogic practices to enrich the therapeutic experience for both client *and* practitioner."   —**Elissa Cobb, MA**, Director of Programs, Phoenix Rising Yoga Therapy; author, *The Forgotten Body*

"This unique contribution to the integration of yoga, psychotherapy, and neuroscience provides an extensive set of practices for healing stress, anxiety, depression, and trauma ... Amy deftly combines breathing, gestures, sounds, imagery, and meditation to address specific therapy issues such as mood, attachment, self esteem, and compassion. It is a pleasure to learn from master teacher, Amy Weintraub."   —**Patricia Gerbarg, MD**, Assistant Professor in Clinical Psychiatry, New York Medical College; co-author, *How to Use Herbs, Nutrients, & Yoga in Mental Health*

"Amy Weintraub is a leader, innovator, and an excellent teacher and writer. In her new book she brings therapists yogic tools to help emotional and physical healing and well-being."   —**Richard Fields, PhD**, Owner/Director, FACES Conferences

Yoga Skills
FOR Therapists

A Norton Professional Book

Yoga Skills
FOR Therapists

Effective Practices
for Mood Management

Amy Weintraub

W. W. NORTON & COMPANY

New York • London

Copyright © 2012 by Amy Weintraub

For information about permission to reproduce selections from this book, write to
Permissions, W. W. Norton & Company, Inc., 500 Fifth Avenue, New York, NY 10110

For information about special discounts for bulk purchases, please contact W. W. Norton
Special Sales at specialsales@wwnorton.com or 800-233-4830

Manufacturing by Quad Graphics, Fairfield
Book design by Carole Desnoes
Production manager: Leeann Graham

Library of Congress Cataloging-in-Publication Data
Weintraub, Amy.
Yoga skills for therapists : effective Practices for mood management / Amy Weintraub.—
1st ed.
    p. cm.
   "A Norton professional book."
   Includes bibliographical references and index.
   ISBN 978-0-393-70717-5 (pbk.)
1. Yoga—Therapeutic use.   I. Title.
RC489.M43 W44 2012
616.89'165—dc23   2011038056
ISBN: 978-0-393-70717-5 (pbk.)

W. W. Norton & Company, Inc., 500 Fifth Avenue, New York, N.Y. 10110
www.wwnorton.com
W. W. Norton & Company Ltd., Castle House, 75/76 Wells Street, London W1T 3QT

1 2 3 4 5 6 7 8 9 0

This book is dedicated to psychotherapists, yoga teachers, and LifeForce Yoga practitioners everywhere, for all the ways you empower and support transformation in the world.

Contents

Acknowledgments

It is my hope that this book might be a manifestation of the knowledge and compassion of all my teachers and students, and that as its writer, I have been a channel for their wisdom and understanding. After the more than 40 years that I have been meditating and the more than 20 years that I have been teaching yoga, I have many dedicated yoga practitioners, teachers, researchers, and therapists to thank. The philosophical foundation of my practice, my teaching, and this book are rooted in the wisdom of the two sages by whom, with grateful pranams, I have been inspired to write this book: Patanjali (2nd c. B.C.E.) and Shankaracharya (9th c. C.E.). I offer my thanks to the dedicated teachers in the Kripalu Yoga lineage, Richard Miller, PhD (iRest), Richard Schwartz, PhD (Internal Family Systems), and to the memory of Nitya Chaitanya Yatri (Advaita Vedanta).

This book would not have been possible without the support of many psychotherapists trained as LifeForce Yoga Practitioners who are integrating yoga-based practices in their therapeutic work. I am indebted to contributions from Deborah Lubetkin, PsyD, LFYP-2; Ann Friedenheim, MA, RYT, LFYP-2; Joe Walter, LCSW, CMFT, RYT, LFYP-2; Laura Orth, LICSW, LFYP-2; Francoise Adan, MD, LFYP; Susan Tebb, PhD, LSW, RYT, LFYP-2; Dory Martin, LCSW, LFYP; Sue Dilsworth, PhD, RYT-500, LFYP-2; Kathryn Shafer, PhD, RYT-500, LFYP-2; Laurie Schaeffer, HN-BC RN, E-RYT 500, LFYP; Mickie Diamond, LCSW, RYT, LFYP; Nancy Nicholson, LCSW, RYT, LFYP; Alexandra Kedrock, LCSW, RYT, LFYP; Patricia Rogers, LFYP; and Cindy Naughton, LMFT, LFYP.

I am also grateful to the distinguished friends and colleagues with whom I've consulted, including the author and research team

Patricia L. Gerbarg, MD, and Richard P. Brown, MD. I am grateful to Ronald D. Siegel, PsyD, for sharing the wisdom he is gathering for his own book, and to Lisa Uebelacker, PhD, for sharing insights from her research on yoga and depression. Special thanks to Richard Miller, PhD, and Robin Carns, ERYT-500, for their contributions to the chapters on yoga nidra and self-inquiry, and for their abiding friendship. A big thank you goes to Jaime Hedlund, RYT, for sharing the story of her deeply moving work with child survivors of sexual abuse and for the outreach work she does with children and their mothers. I'm grateful to Dan L. Newman, LPC, for his contribution and kindness during the writing of this book. I am indebted to meticulous and generous Mark Hurwich who helped me proof these pages and offered his unconditional support.

I offer a special bow to my dear friend Joy Bennett, LFYP-2, ERYT-500, the yoga therapist who contributed several case studies from the breadth of her yoga therapy practice, and to friend and colleague Felicity Boyer, MBA, RYT, LFYP-2, for her contribution and ongoing support.

Both this book and I owe a great deal to Elena "Rose" Kress, CYT 500, LFYP-2, who, as LifeForce Yoga Healing Institute program manager, has assisted me in keeping our many other projects going throughout the writing process. The photographs of hands in mudras and body parts in pranayama breathing exercises and poses were taken by Rose. She has carefully checked the manuscript for Sanskrit spelling errors and misstatements. I am grateful for her loyalty and support.

Finally, I was blessed to have Andrea Costella Dawson as my careful, meticulous, curious, trustworthy, and kind editor at W. W. Norton, for which I am ever grateful.

Yoga Skills

FOR Therapists

INTRODUCTION

The inspiration for this book actually dates back 4,000 years. That's how long yogis have used the laboratory of their bodies to discover and refine practices that promote balance and ease, not just in the physical body but in the emotional and mental bodies as well. *Yoga Skills for Therapists* is a compendium of these yoga-based practices that are specific to mood management. The practices are drawn from my own recovery from an anxiety-based depression more than 20 years ago, my studies in yogic science through the lens of several traditions, the research I have reviewed and coauthored, and my direct work with thousands of students and clients for the last 20 years.

Yoga Skills is an easy beginners' guide to the practices I teach the psychotherapists and health professionals who take my LifeForce Yoga Practitioner Training. LifeForce Yoga is hatha yoga plain and simple. It doesn't really need a name, but in this day and age, when there are so many ways of practicing that are called yoga, it's important to identify a practice that is intentionally designed to work with and manage the mood. The practice is adapted to the individual, so he or she can move into a balanced emotional, mental, and physical state of equanimity and self-awareness.

My own journey toward recovery from anxiety-based depression began in 1970 with a daily meditation practice. In 1989 I began to practice Kripalu Yoga, and it was that daily embodied practice joined to the breath that freed me from depression. Since then, I have studied with yoga masters and meditation teachers in the United States and India and have done extensive research to develop a practice that weaves ancient classical and Tantric practices with current scientific understanding of their benefits and contraindications. I have called this practice LifeForce Yoga so that students know that they will be integrating sound, breath, hand gestures, meditation techniques, and self-inquiry, whether or not they practice postures. Those who take the training learn that LifeForce Yoga is a practice of compassion that creates a big enough container to embrace and accept all the dualities of mood.

These practitioners are among the approximately 16 million Americans and countless others internationally who are currently experiencing the benefits of yoga, and perhaps you are among them too. Like those who take my training, you may have become aware of the shift in your own mood that yoga engenders. Like them, you may already have felt the self-efficacy that the power to manage your mood through yoga provides. Or you may have observed an improvement in a client's mood after she enrolled in a yoga class and began to regularly practice the emotional and biochemical self-regulating strategies yoga bestows.

And now, you may be reading this book because you would like to introduce your clients to strategies that they can use to feel better about themselves and the world. You may have heard from a colleague about how much easier it is for your clients to focus and to talk about their feelings after beginning a session with a simple yogic breathing exercise. The therapists and other health professionals who work with me are excited about the simple somatic tools gleaned from the timeless teachings of yoga that they can share with their clients in a clinical setting—no mat required. This guidebook not only makes them available to you but shares many of the ways therapists are comfortably introducing yoga skills to those they serve.

HOW TO USE THIS BOOK

Yoga Skills provides you with simple practices for a clinical setting such as breathing exercises, easy meditations, and hand gestures called *mudras* that empower your clients to self-regulate, increasing feelings of self-efficacy and control, while at the same time enhancing your therapeutic relationship. These practices do not require a yoga mat. They differ from what you might experience in an ordinary yoga class in that they don't require you or your client to understand alignment principles or to practice postures. Although you don't need prior yoga experience to practice and then teach these basic skills to your clients, my hope is that you will be inspired to develop your own regular practice. Not only will your own practice of these yoga skills bring more ease and balance into your daily life, but you will feel the effects firsthand before teaching them to your clients.

The yoga practices described and illustrated here have been the foundation of yoga for thousands of years, long before postures like warriors and downward-facing dog and sequences like sun salutations entered the hatha yoga lexicon in the 19th century. These timeless practices have been handed down from master to student, some of them likely for 5,000 years, before they were written down in yoga practice texts like the *Hatha Yoga Pradipika*, the *Gheranda Samhita*, and the *Goraksha Samita*, all thought to have been written between the 6th and the 15th centuries. These simple but profound yoga skills will offer you and your clients a way to begin a session with a clear and centered mind and an open heart. They will provide you with tools to come back into balance in and between sessions, and they will deepen the therapeutic work you do together. You will want to share this book with those you serve so that your clients can follow the practices you recommend at home.

Each section explains and shows a practice and its application to a particular mood or mental state. The many stories and anecdotes presented throughout the book are from therapists I have inter-viewed directly, and will give you ideas for introducing the tech-nique to your clients and what to expect when they practice it regularly. You may wish to read this through to absorb the prac-tices offered and then practice them at home before offering them to clients. After you have read and practiced the strategies in this book, keep the book in your office as a reference tool. There will be abundant opportunities to pull it off the shelf to help one client bring herself back into balance, or to teach another something to lift his mood, or even to clear your own space between clients and phone calls and documentation for third-party payers.

With this book in your and your clients' hands, you can more confidently expect clients to practice at home. You will find that you are enjoying your work more, because as you teach these mood-managing strategies, you are practicing them too.

CHAPTER 1

WHY YOGA NOW?

The practice of yoga is much more than the postures, called asanas, that most yoga schools teach. There is a rich, nearly 5,000-year-old tradition of yoga that does not even include the poses that we traditionally think of as yoga. The ancient yogis understood that emotional and mental well-being were possible through yoga practices that did not require a mat, blocks, straps, eye pillows, or even cushions. The practices in this book are not New Age inventions, nor are they made up by me and other contemporary yoga teachers. They hark back to yoga's roots, and the beauty of these timeless teachings is that they are perfectly suited to the consultation room.

YOGA AS A COMPLEMENT TO PSYCHOTHERAPY

Debbie Lubetkin, a clinical psychologist in northern New Jersey, is using such a timeless practice as she works with Suzanne,*a client with a severe eating disorder who presented her problem as "wanting to control what is sometimes uncontrollable." Suzanne was so anxious at the beginning of treatment that Dr. Lubetkin introduced a simple yoga breathing practice in the first session to provide her with a felt sense of how she actually did have more control than she believed—that she could actually induce a sense

*All names and identifying details of clients have been changed in this book.

of comfort. "Her reaction was 'Wow!'" says Dr. Lubetkin. Suzanne was relaxed enough to begin the work of therapy during the very first session.

The work of therapy can hardly begin in earnest when the client's mind is racing and jumping from thought to thought. In such a case, neither linear thought nor emotional awareness can find a crack in the wall of chaos the client presents. The practices in this book will help you and your client break through the wall so that both of you can settle in for a more focused and productive session. Nor will therapy be therapeutic if your client is shut down and out of touch with feelings. Distrust, a history of trauma, anger, depression, or court-mandated sessions can all present another kind of wall that is challenging to scale. The practices in this book can begin to dissolve the wall, so that it becomes translucent, like a screen behind which light can be discerned and trust can grow.

That point was brought home when I began a class in the juvenile detention center in Tucson, and the only time available was at 12:30 P.M., right after the girls had eaten a carbohydrate-laden lunch. Not the best time to practice yoga. When the girls shuffled in, their faces were expressionless, and their eyes were cast down. I called it full-belly yoga. We had to confine ourselves to the calming breathing, mantra, and mudra practices described in Chapters 4, 6, and 7, and we couldn't do the more energizing breathing practices most suited to shining a light through the darkness of spirit (the mood-elevating practices found in Chapter 5), yet the 12- to 18-year-olds were calmer and more open to their feelings after yoga class. "Missy, look at my baby," said a 15-year-old child, holding up a picture of her 1-year-old daughter, being raised by her grandmother. Soon the therapist assigned to the unit noticed the change in the girls and asked that the class be moved to just before group therapy at 4:00 P.M. to take best advantage of the girls' increased focus and willingness to talk about their feelings.

There are numerous no-mat yoga tools that can facilitate and enhance the nonverbal work of therapy, such as building trust in the relationship, along with the verbal work. There are four distinct ways in which yoga can profoundly support your therapeutic work.

First, there is the creation of the therapeutic bond, the safe and sacred space where therapy will take place. As Bruce Wampold (2001) suggests in his meta-analysis of over 400 manualized treatments for depression, the greatest predictor of a beneficial outcome for the client is not the therapeutic modality utilized, but the relationship between client and therapist. Yoga can assist in establishing and maintaining the therapeutic bond in its offering of rituals and practices, of which there are many, including the lighting of a candle, the use of a hand gesture called a *mudra*, a simple yoga breath called a *pranayama*, an image of sanctuary or of peace called a *bhavana*, a soothing universal tone called a *mantra*, or a cleansing breath called a *kriya*, from which the client's intention for the session or for his life may naturally reveal itself, or a combination of any or all of these ancient practices.

All of these simple rituals can soften the heart, creating a tender bond between therapist and client. Buddhist teacher and writer Sharon Salzburg talks about asking a psychiatrist at a party what he felt was the agent of change in therapy. She says that he thought for a moment and then declared, "I would have to say, it's the love in the room." Simply believing that your client has everything he needs within him to heal, which is the foundational belief of all yoga, simply believing in the wholeness of your client and communicating that to him may enhance that "love in the room" and foster the therapeutic bond.

Second, there is a slow invitation to move back into a felt sense of living in the body, without ever having to say so directly. This begins with the subtle cueing the teacher or therapist offers to her client, allowing him to acknowledge sensation in his face, for example, or his hands after guiding a practice, without ever saying, "It's safe to feel your body," a concept your client's mind may immediately resist.

Third, there are the many practices in this book that are based in the body and yet gently begin to still and focus the mind for the work of therapy.

Fourth, yoga has a tradition of holding poses, sometimes until the body begins to tremble. There are also dynamic meditation practices that lead the client to shake for a period of time. The ancient yogis made the assumption that by vigorously shaking, we are releasing tension and intrinsic memory stored in the body-mind. This theory underlies many therapeutic modalities, including the work of somatic psychotherapists like Peter Levine, Pat Ogden, David Berceli, Deirdre Fay, and others. Phoenix Rising Yoga Therapy is a yoga modality that is based on this principle. Some yoga traditions include a practice of long therapeutic holding of a pose, grounded in the assumption that the energetic and physical release that may occur has the potential to dissolve even the unremembered trauma memories still held in the body.

It is not within the scope of this book to cover the therapeutic use of holding a pose, as this requires a skilled facilitator, trained in the management of catharsis and the occasional flashback that might occur. In addition, this kind of work is not recommended for those in the acute stages of post-traumatic stress disorder (PTSD). It is more than enough and in fact quite a gift to simply cue to sensations as described above, allowing the client to reclaim a body she may have abandoned during trauma.

All four principles were engaged when Nancy Nicholson, a clinical social worker and yoga teacher in Charlotte, North Carolina, worked with a thirty-four-year-old client. "Elizabeth" was an accomplished professional, smart, quick witted, competitive, and attractive, with a reputation of being a leader in the community. At their first session, Elizabeth could not look Nancy in the eye for more than a few seconds, had very shallow breathing, and constantly moved her hands while speaking rapidly and with great wit. "She changed the subject if we got too close to her heart," says

Nancy. Yet, through a simple ritual to establish a "safe container" for their work together, Elizabeth was able to express a clear intention, called a *sankalpa* in Sanskrit, for freedom from her anxiety. In that first session, Nancy established the safe container by means of the second principle, sensing the body, and the third principle, focusing the mind. She led Elizabeth through a simple yoga breathing exercise and then invited her to breathe a single channel of freedom through whatever anxiety she was feeling in that moment. Elizabeth visibly relaxed and seemed more grounded in her body, but still did not return Nancy's gaze.

Elizabeth had been sexually abused by her grandfather, had eating disorders for many years, and had tried therapy a number of times previously. During their ongoing sessions of talk therapy, they continued to focus on using the breath and gentle yoga movements to help Elizabeth feel calm and more comfortable in her body. After a time, Elizabeth felt safe enough in her body that Nancy introduced practices based on the fourth principle—body awareness exercises related to holding emotions and some standing breathing with larger body movements for the release of anger, always with assurance that Elizabeth was in control of what and how much she did. Throughout the three years of Elizabeth's therapy, Nancy taught her relaxation techniques, like yoga nidra, described in Chapter 9. In their last meeting, Elizabeth described herself as "calm, with a deep breath" as she looked Nancy squarely in the eyes.

ARE YOU ALREADY DOING YOGA?

The principles of yoga complement the ultimate goals of therapy: self-awareness, self-acceptance, self-efficacy, self-regulation, and whatever individual goals you and your clients may hold for their optimum well-being. As we explore the ways in which these goals are supported by yoga practices in the chapters that follow, you may at times find yourself saying, "But this is what I already do." Exactly! If you're reading this book, you likely understand the importance of regulating the body to regulate the emotions and may have been using some form of somatic intervention for years. What you may not know is that this somatic intervention may have originated in the timeless teachings of yoga. For thousands of years, yogis have used strategies to balance the body-mind that look a lot like contemporary therapy. Within the yoga traditions, you will find aspects of cognitive-behavioral therapy, dialectic behavior therapy, coherence therapy, acceptance and commitment therapy, internal family systems therapy, and even treatment aspects of eye movement desensitization and reprocessing, emotional freedom technique, and other forms of energy psychology.

When you think of yoga, you might imagine young, flexible bodies executing complex stretches, but did you know that there are many practices that don't require a yoga mat and can be done in your office chair? If you are a therapist who practices one of the many body-based psychotherapies and are already comfortable inviting your client to stand or lie down, there is an abundance of yoga-based movements, meditations, and breathing practices that can be done from all three positions, right in your office.

You may currently be integrating yoga-inspired mind-body strategies without even knowing it. If you use imagery with your clients, intention setting, breathing practices, mindfulness, or movement, what I am suggesting in this book is not so very different from what you are already doing. Alexandra Kedrock is a clinical social worker in Norfolk, Virginia, who had been using many of these strategies with clients before she became a yoga teacher. She might say to a client, "Where is that in your body? What does it look like?" Then she "finds a way to dissipate the hurtful feeling with either imagery or breath." Like many of you, Alexandra was also already using movement in her therapy practice. For example, even before her yoga training, she might have invited a client to stand, in order to feel more grounded, and to imagine roots moving deep into the earth.

The practices that begin in the next chapter can add new somatic strategies from the yoga tradition to your toolbox or may actually change the way you practice. One thing is for sure: If you guide your clients through a practice or two suggested in these pages during a session, you will feel more focused and more relaxed, along with your client, and I'll bet you'll have a lot more fun.

PSYCHOLOGICAL EFFECTS OF YOGA ON & OFF THE MAT

Often clients come to therapy already practicing some form of hatha yoga. (Hatha is the term that embraces all "physical force" styles of yoga, so whether it's Ashtanga, Bikram, Kripalu, Viniyoga, Iyengar, or any one of the numerous schools of yoga, if it's on the mat, it's hatha.) It may be that they have found a practice that supports their emotional well-being—that meets their current mood and constitution and moves them into balance. Or they may have chosen a practice that exacerbates their already over-driven propensities. For example, suppose you suggest to an anxious type A personality, diagnosed with hypertension, that he enroll in a yoga class. He might be drawn to try a fiery, vigorous style of yoga offered at his health and fitness club, or a class where the emphasis on perfecting difficult poses could appeal to his competitive nature. However, if he doesn't slow his practice down, he's likely to feel as agitated at the completion of his yoga session as when he began. If there is too much emphasis on perfecting the pose, despite feelings of accomplishment that may arise, there's also a risk of activating feelings of failure. A rigid approach to getting it right is more likely to engage the sympathetic nervous system, even as it may provoke feelings of shame about not being good enough.

Although even yoga practiced in a driven and compulsive way can produce physical and psychological benefits, the most psychologically efficacious practice is slower, cultivating a mindful attention to the breath and to the sensations in the body. Susi Hately, a therapeutic yoga teacher and teacher trainer, puts it this way:

When a teacher guides in a more relaxed, slow, and deliberate way, respiration and heart rate slow down, and as a result the whole nervous system calms down and settles. This is a parasympathetic response where not only does the mind quiet, but the myofascial structures start to let go. This mindful process has, quite literally, a different physiological effect than a rigid approach. (2010, p. 15)

The same dynamic applies off the mat and in the consultation room. For example, you could lead a fiery breathing practice that might leave your client even more agitated than when he arrived. The yoga tools in this book are grouped into practices that are more stimulating and those that are more calming. But the best way to avoid an overstimulating effect is to pause and check in. After leading one of the practices suggested and then cueing your client to sense deeply into the area of strongest sensation (e.g., face, fingertips, palms of the hands), ask your client to describe what she is sensing in her body and as she does so, observe her affect. Not only is this good information for you in terms of how to proceed, but you are helping her cultivate her own capacity to observe, without reaction, what is occurring in the moment. For some clients for whom it has not felt safe to live in the body after a traumatizing event or a long history of abuse, the ability to stay present with what is arising, to actually notice the body again without numbing out, may be one of the greatest gifts you can offer. If yoga is practiced in this compassionate and self-observing way, the psychological benefits are enhanced.

YOGA MEETS TRAUMA

Therapeutic yoga approaches the emotions from the doorway of the body, or, more precisely, from the residue left in the body by trauma and loss and the everyday challenges of daily life. It meets the constrictions held and helps the client release them, often without words. This can be especially valuable when trauma has occurred preverbally or when trauma memories are stored intrinsically and cannot be recalled chronologically. This is also often the case in shock trauma, when the fight-or-flight hormone cortisol floods the limbic brain and disrupts the natural memory-arranging function of the hippocampus.

In developmental trauma, when a pattern of abuse has inclined the client to dissociate, often the memory of repeated trauma is there, but devoid of the painful emotions one would associate with the events. Yoga works bilaterally, integrating the emotions back into left-brain narrative in the case of developmental trauma, and integrating a more linear left-brain narrative into the emotionally laden intrinsic memories that accompany shock trauma. In either case, yoga, with its cultivation of an observing mind, its release of chronic tension stored in the body, and its many techniques using breathing and sound that help clients access the wellspring of well-being that exists beneath the effects of the trauma, can provide trauma survivors a way to feel safe in their bodies and safe in the world. (See the next chapter for some general guidelines about introducing yoga to traumatized patients.)

Bessel Van der Kolk, founder and medical director of the Trauma Center in Brookline, Massachusetts, and a pioneer in the trauma field, has said that he will not work with a trauma survivor who is not practicing yoga. "If you really want to help a traumatized person, you have to work with core physiological states, and then the mind will start changing" (Van der Kolk, interviewed by Wylie, 2004a, p. 36). In an article published in the *Annals of the New York Academy of Sciences,* Van der Kolk (2006) discussed a small study conducted at the Trauma Center that compared eight 75-minute yoga sessions to eight sessions of group dialectical behavior therapy, the therapeutic model used at the Trauma Center. Only the yoga group showed an increase in heart rate variability (HRV) and a decrease in the frequency of intrusive thoughts and the severity of hyperarousal symptoms. At the Trauma Center and in his training for psychotherapists and other health professionals, yoga is an integrated part of the treatment plan.

IS YOGA A SCIENCE?

Yoga seems to affect all areas and systems in the brain through biochemical reactions that increase HRV, thereby balancing the autonomic nervous system. Evidence has shown a reduction in cortisol secretions and an increase in gamma-amniobutyric acid (GABA) levels, which reduces limbic brain activity (Streeter, 2010). The limbic region is the social-emotional-motivational nexus of the brain and the amygdala is the key. When trauma and loss occur early in life, the amygdala, which encodes negative emotions like fear, anger, and sadness into long-term implicit memory, becomes hypersensitive (Badenoch, 2011). The amygdala is overactivated by stress. Those who have been traumatized are often in a perpetual state of amygdala overactivation, so much so that the amygdala begins to shrink. This happens because repeated exposure to stress actually kills off our neurons! I joke with the professionals in my training sessions that they are becoming amygdala whisperers.

On a biochemical and physiological level, previous research has shown that yoga relaxes chronic muscle tension, restores natural diaphragmatic breathing, improves oxygen absorption and carbon dioxide elimination, increases alpha and theta brain waves, and regulates the thalamus at an optimum level. (The job of the thalamus is to send information to the insula cortex, activating the poor, overstimulated amygdala.) Certain techniques stimulate vagal nerve activity, which has been shown to be effective in the treatment of major depression. The vagus nerve runs from the brain stem to the colon, regulating all our basic survival functions along its path, including heartbeat, muscle movement, breathing, and digestion. This wandering nerve transmits a variety of chemicals to and from the brain. Scientists don't know exactly why stimulation positively effects mood, but it is reasonable to say that it harks back to the importance of the body–mind connection. Yoga practices increase the bioavailability of oxygen and glucose in the brain, which are the building blocks for the production of neurotransmitters. Recent studies are also demonstrating a wide range of psychological benefits, including the elevation of mood, the cultivation of equanimity in the face of life's challenges, the development of greater self-awareness, increased feelings of self-efficacy, increased feelings of self-compassion, better management of bipolar disorder, greater access to feelings, the release of repressed emotions stored in the body, and the increased ability to self-regulate. We can say this because of the work of pioneering researchers who are validating what yogis have understood for thousands of years.

Most familiar to therapists are the studies that document the efficacy of mindfulness practices in treating mood disorders as delivered in the 8-week Mindfulness-Based Stress Reduction (MBSR) program developed by John Kabat-Zinn and his former colleagues at the University of Massachusetts. This program includes a yoga movement portion as well as a body-scan relaxation, similar to what yogis call yoga nidra. An MBSR training for survivors of sexual trauma at the University of Maryland Center for Integrative Medicine that, in addition to meditation, includes gentle yoga has shown a dramatic decrease in symptoms of depression, PTSD, and anxiety after the 8-week intervention. Most significantly, in the 24-week follow-up, gains remained at nearly the postintervention rate (Kimbrough, Magyari, Langenberg, Chesney, & Berman, 2010).

Other studies, familiar to many therapists, were done by Herbert Benson and his colleagues at Harvard, where since the early 1970s research has shown the efficacy of mantra-based meditation or, as Benson calls it, the relaxation response. Therapists may also know of Belleruth Naparstek's guided imagery work and the studies that have shown its efficacy in working with trauma (Eller, 1999; Giedt, 1997). The ancient yogis called the visualization of a supporting image from the past or the future a *bhavana*. Through oral transmission from master to student, they have been teaching such imagery and relaxation techniques for thousands of years.

But a new kind of yoga research is on the horizon—which therapists may not be aware of—that makes use of biochemical analysis, brain scans, and physiological measurements of stress. This research is pioneered by eminent scientists like Shirley Telles, director of research at Patanjali Yogpeeth in Haridwar and the Indian Council of Medical Research Center in Bangalore, India, who has published over 120 studies in peer-reviewed journals; Richard Davidson at the University of Wisconsin; Sat Bir Khalsa at Harvard; Sarah Lazar and her colleagues at Harvard; Luciano Bernardi at the University of Pavia in Italy; and Richard Brown and Patricia Gerberg at Columbia University and New York Medical College. These scientists and their findings have paved the way for larger government and military grants to study the effects of a variety of yoga-based protocols in the treatment of PTSD, depression, and other diagnostic categories.

Based on these scientists' earlier groundbreaking research and previous research of his own, Lorenzo Cohen, director of the Integrative Medicine Program at the MD Anderson Cancer Center in Houston and grandson of yoga luminary Vanda Scarvelli, is using a $4.5 million grant from the National Institutes of Health (NIH) to fund a large randomized controlled study of yoga practice in women with cancer. His current research is based on the evidence that psychological stress is a predictor of mortality in breast cancer patients. In animal studies, mice injected with tumors fared better when given propanol to block the stress hormone norepinephrine as compared to mice without propanol, whose tumors metastasized. Based on the theory that yoga also reduces norepinephrine and therefore strengthens immunity to stress, Dr. Cohen and his team used various yoga styles, including Tibetan yoga and a hatha yoga protocol developed in collaboration with the Vivekananda Kendra in Bangalore. The findings are validating his thesis that a decrease in depressive symptoms impacts long-term survival rates in breast cancer patients.

Cohen's 2004 study used the Tibetan yoga protocol with lymphoma patients and found improvement in sleep disturbances, a reduction in dark thoughts, and symptom reduction posttreatment (Cohen, Warneke, Fouladi, Rodriguez, & Chaoul-Reich, 2004). His 2010 study, in collaboration with the Vivekananda Kendra Yoga Research Foundation in Bangalore, found a reduction in the stress hormone cortisol and an increase in "finding meaning in life" 3 months after the yoga intervention (Chandwani et al., 2010). What is illuminating about this increase in "meaning" is that those who measured highest in "finding meaning in life" at 3 months showed a higher incidence of intrusive thoughts at 1 month. This could indicate that yoga allows and cultivates a welcoming attitude to all that is arising in the mind, including negative and intrusive thoughts. Might it be possible that in the process of bringing the sludge to the surface, yoga also encourages qualities of acceptance, balance, and even joy? Could it be that those who remain in denial of their fears and fight to keep negative thoughts at bay may be contributing to their own psychological stress, which as stated above is a predictor of mortality among breast cancer patients?

Ronald Siegel, assistant clinical professor at the Harvard Medical School, might agree. In his forthcoming book with Christopher Germer, *Wisdom and Compassion in Psychotherapy: Deepening Mindfulness in Clinical Practice*, he writes about a common theme that has emerged from the 20 prominent therapists he has interviewed—the most important role the therapist can play is not about fixing or solving problems but helping clients tolerate problems in their lives that include uncertainty and pain (Siegel, personal communication, April 2011). The wisdom traditions of the East help us cultivate an observing mind, what yogis call the witness or seer. When difficult things happen, as they invariably do, we can respond with greater equanimity and less reactivity.

This is one of the assumptions underlying a large, randomized, controlled NIH-funded 4-year trial underway at Brown University and Butler Hospital in Providence, Rhode Island. "Yoga students are often taught to attend to thoughts and emotions during practice in a noncritical fashion," says research and clinical psychologist Lisa Uebelacker, the principle investigator. "As students learn this potentially new way of approaching themselves and the world, students may become more mindful in daily life. The ability to be mindful may subvert depressive hopelessness by increasing focus on the present (rather than ruminating about the past or worrying about the future) and decreasing self-criticism" (Uebelacker, personal communication, May 2011). Uebelacker and her colleagues are looking at the effects of a yoga program on individuals who are taking antidepressants for major depressive disorder yet still not feeling fully recovered. The yoga program consists of a mindful, meditative, and gentle in-class style of yoga combined with home practice that includes LifeForce Yoga videos (see Chapter 11). The control group will take a program that involves education about health-related topics, such as nutrition, sleep, or exercise. According to Uebelacker, "the study will evaluate these two interventions to determine whether and how they improve symptoms and quality of life (i.e., social functioning, work/role functioning, physical functioning, and pain) amongst individuals with an illness that can be chronic and/or life-threatening (major depression). A secondary goal of this project involves determining whether cortisol levels and biomarkers of inflammation mediate the effects of the interventions on depression." As a consultant on this study, I see firsthand the enthusiasm of the researchers and their yoga teacher colleagues in preparing the study design and manual. These investigators have moved slowly, step by step, building on earlier studies done by the pioneering researchers and on their own preliminary trials.

The early research also supports investigators like epidemiologist Kim Innes, associate professor at West Virginia University and the University of Virginia, who has completed seven studies, funded by a National Center for Complementary and Alternative Medicine (NCCAM) grant that looked at the effects of yoga as an intervention for the prevention and treatment of cardiovascular disease, diabetes, Parkinson's disease, and other conditions in postmenopausal women and older adults. She is also investigating the application and usefulness of yoga for adults with cognitive impairment (and their caregivers), osteoarthritis, and other related diseases. Although she was testing for other improvements like balance and gait, she included psychosocial measurements in her studies and in all cases, she found improvements in mood and sleep and a reduction of stress (Alexander et al., 2010; Innes, Selfe, & Taylor, 2008; Innes, Selfe, & Vishnu, 2010; Innes & Vincent, 2007; Selfe & Innes, 2009; Taylor, Goehler, Galper, Innes, & Bourguignon, 2010).

In many yoga research studies that focus on diabetes, low back pain, cancer, heart disease, and other physiological imbalances, the researchers also look at changes in patient mood following the yoga intervention. For example, Robert Saper, director of the Integrative Medicine program at the Boston Medical Center, who is studying the efficacy of yoga for low back pain in underserved minority populations, addresses the psychological dimensions of the condition. People suffering from low back pain often exhibit fear and avoidance behaviors, limiting their movements, which can make the condition worse. When patients become sedentary, muscles can atrophy and weight gain can place additional stress on the painful area. Untreated low back pain reduces levels of gamma-aminobutyric acid (GABA), a neurotransmitter that when low is implicated in depression. Saper's current research reflects positive changes in mood, a decrease in fear and avoidance behaviors, and increase in GABA levels following yoga practice (Saper et al., 2009).

Stress researchers Janice Kiecolt-Glaser and her colleagues at Ohio State University have shown that regular yoga practice reduces levels of circulating inflammatory markers, a known risk factor in cardiovascular disease, asthma, and depression (Kiecolt-Glaser et al., 2010). The investigators are continuing their research with one of the largest yoga and cancer studies to date. According

to Marcia Miller, the yoga teacher who designed the yoga protocol for breast cancer surviviors, the women are given 12 weeks of
twice-weekly classes with sequences designed to maximize circu-
lation to the upper chest and armpit area, and to improve overall immunity with simple inversions and relaxing restorative poses.
"I have been so inspired to work with these women," says Marcia.
"In the 3 months we have had together they have a renewed confidence in their bodies and their abilities to make good choices for
themselves based on their needs of the moment. They have hope
for their futures as they stay focused in the now."

What is exciting about these studies is that they are using bio-
marker measurements as well as the more traditional psychosocial
measures like the Hamilton Scale, the Beck Depression Inventory,
and the Profile of Mood States. For example, recent studies at the
University of Pennsylvania, Boston University, and elsewhere have
shown that the practice of yoga decreases cortisol, the stress hormone, while increasing GABA levels and HRV. Low GABA levels and low HRV are associated with both depression and anxiety
(Streeter et al., 2007). A 2010 study by the same Boston University
team, led by Chris Streeter, not only demonstrated an increase
in GABA levels among yoga participants over a matched group
that practiced walking, but a self-reported elevation of mood and
reduced symptoms of anxiety over the walkers (Streeter et al., 2010).

A small but comprehensive study that used an Iyengar Yoga protocol, conducted by David Shapiro and his colleagues at UCLA,
measured both biochemical and psychosocial markers for depression. The researchers found that of the 17 completers, all diagnosed
with unipolar depression in partial remission, 11 were in complete
remission after the intervention (Shapiro et al., 2007).

Yoga has been shown to trigger brain-derived neurotrophic factor
(BDNF), a neurotrophic factor required for neurons to communicate,
which helps us continue to learn and grow from our experiences.
Some studies have shown that people practicing yogic breathing can
have a rate of recovery from major depression as high as 73%.

The expansion of yoga research is fueled by two major sources, the first of which is the U.S. military. Because of the high rates of suicide, PTSD, and depression among soldiers returning from Iraq and Afghanistan, government sources have awarded grants to support nonmedical research, mostly at large Veterans Administration (VA) hospitals, like the study of iRest, the yoga nidra protocol fine tuned by psychologist and yoga master Richard Miller as a treatment for PTSD, currently underway at the Miami VA. As I write this, 83 active studies funded by NIH and NCCAM are using yoga as a treatment modality.

Many more studies are in the pipeline, funded by alternative sources like the Institute for Extraordinary Living at Kripalu Center or by passionate postdoctoral students, eager to demonstrate to the world the healing power of yoga that they have discovered on their own yoga mats. A number of multisite studies that will compare the efficacy of psychotherapy with and without a yoga component are seeking funding as I write.

In addition to working with established research institutions like the Mayo Clinic and Brown University, I consult with a number of doctoral candidates and postdoc researchers currently working on the efficacy of yoga for improving mood. These passionate researchers are sometimes funding their own studies or competing for NIH student grants as they complete their advanced academic degrees. Some of these studies will show up as poster presentations at national conferences and some will find their way into prestigious peer-reviewed journals.

Such is the case for research currently underway that examines the effects of the LifeForce Yoga protocol on mood. The first study, which included 94 general subjects not isolated for mood, was published in the peer-reviewed *International Journal of Yoga Therapy* in 2008. The Beck Depression Inventory and the Profile of Mood States were used to measure mood before the introduction of the yoga protocol, then 2 weeks after an intensive 5-day training in the protocol, and then again 2 months later. According to one of the study's authors, Shannon Bennett, between the first measurement (before the 5-day LifeForce Yoga program) and the second (2 weeks after learning it), participants reported a 64% decrease in total mood disturbance, which continued to decrease when measurements were taken 2 months later (Bennett, Weintraub, & Khalsa, 2008).

We are currently looking at the effect of this protocol along with psychotherapy on mild to moderately depressed clients who score between 7 and 28 on the Beck Depression Inventory, and comparing it to a matched group doing psychotherapy alone.

YOGA AS HOLISTIC HEALING

There are research challenges to be sure, because, as evidenced by this book, yoga is comprised of a multitude of tools for mood management. Although a reductionist medical-model measurement of a particular breath or posture can provide useful information regarding which yoga treatments might affect which conditions, yoga restores balance on all levels of our individual existence, including the physical, emotional, mental, and spirit bodies in which we live. Yogis refer to this holistic approach as the *kosha* model or the sheaths of our existence. For example, for a client who is carrying the slumped posture of her depressed mood, we may suggest that she place her feet flat on the floor and invite her to straighten her spine and even place a folded blanket or a cushion behind her back, as we lead her through an even pattern of inhalation and exhalation, while guiding her to observe the sensation arising. In this way, we are not only addressing her physical posture but are also affecting her emotions and thoughts, and perhaps beginning to impact the beliefs she holds about herself and the world. Timothy McCall, medical editor of *Yoga Journal* and the author of *Yoga as Medicine: The Yogic Prescription for Health and Healing*, puts it this way:

Yoga is holistic, and when you only measure it in reductionist fashion, you're always going to underestimate its true value. Yoga isn't designed to affect single variables or single disease states the way drugs are, but to change practitioners physically, mentally, emotionally, and spiritually, in ways that Yoga believes are deeply interconnected. Yoga appears to make various systems of the body—respiratory, nervous, cardiovascular, immunological, and so on—work better. Single measures like cortisol, cholesterol, and bone mineral density are never going to capture that, though the fact that improvements in each of these measures has been documented in clinical studies is valuable. (McGonigal, 2009, p. 145)

Therapists and their clients who are already using these yoga tools don't need to wait for peer-reviewed studies to know that they are feeling better. They are, like Joy Bennett, a yoga therapist in Providence, Rhode Island, recovering from mood disorders and sustaining their optimum mental health with their practice. Joy had spent the better part of her life struggling with a genetic predisposition to depression. "Like many of my relatives," she says, "I also happen to be wired for anxiety."

After years of emotional upheaval, she discovered yoga in her 40s. "[It was] the best thing that could have happened to me. It's said that yoga is a transformational process, and I learned firsthand just how true that is. A regular practice of yoga brought me out of the brain fog and tears." Later, in her 50s, Joy began experiencing panic attacks she associates with the hormonal changes of menopause. "I was a yoga teacher by this time. I wasn't supposed to feel this way!" Joy added what she was learning in her training as a LifeForce Yoga Practitioner to her daily practice. "I learned that [by] stimulating the chakras through seed sounds and mudras, I could balance the hormones of the endocrine system." She added the daily practice of the LifeForce Chakra Clearing Meditation to her routine (see Chapter 7), which incorporates sound and hand gestures called mudras. "I kept up with the chakra clearing consistently—in the shower, no less! I combined this with a few other breathing techniques. Between the steam and the sounding, I was feeling mighty clear when I toweled down and started my day feeling focused and fresh!"

Maybe you can relate to Joy's dilemma. Perhaps there are times when you say to yourself, but I'm a psychotherapist. I'm not supposed to feel this way. The practices we will explore together in the following chapters will allow you to remain in balance, welcoming whatever arises in your own life, without judgment, just as you are helping your clients to tolerate the inevitable stress and loss in their lives. In the next chapter, we will explore the basic principles that can help you feel more comfortable as you begin to integrate yoga into your personal and your clinical practice.

CHAPTER 2

BASIC YOGA PRINCIPLES & PREPARATIONS

Most yoga lineages ground the theory and practice of their tradition in a book written in about 200 A.D., based on an oral tradition that had likely been handed down from master to student for thousands of years. There are hundreds of translations and commentaries of this book, called *The Yoga Sutras*. The sage Patanjali is credited with the compilation of the 200 stanzas, referred to as *sutras*, a word that literally means thread. The second chapter of the *Yoga Sutras* is about the actual practice of yoga, and yet no yoga postures are included. The only instruction is that *asana*, which literally means "seat" for meditation, be "steady and comfortable" or "joyful," depending on which translation you read. What this means is that you and your client, sitting in a steady and comfortable way in your consultation room, are already practicing yoga.

Joe Walter, a psychotherapist for over 30 years, now incorporates yoga into his practice in Slinger, Wisconsin, and relies on this "steady and comfortable" definition of asana when he introduces yoga into a session. He might start a session by inviting his client into "seated mountain pose," suggesting a straight spine and a lift to the crown of the head so that breath might flow more easily (Figure 2.1). For someone in the slumped posture of depression, where the lungs are too compressed to take a full diaphragmatic breath, a simple postural adjustment may invite a mood shift.

Figure 2.1. Joe Walter, MA, with client in Seated Mountain Pose

YOGA PHILOSOPHY: INSPIRATION TO HEAL

The tradition in the sacred texts of Indian philosophy is that the essential teaching is spoken first and that is all that the truly gifted student needs to hear. The rest of the text is elaboration and explication of the "right view." The first stanza or sutra therefore is the essence of what follows. Here is the first sutra in the chapter about yoga practice (Pada 2) in Patanjali's *Yoga Sutras*: "*Tapas svadhyaya Ishvara-pranidhana kriya yoga.*" This is the foundational instruction, and it is indeed a prescription for optimum mental health. It is a formula for achieving "union in action" (*kriya yoga*), action that is clearly aligned with one's authentic sense of self. In this sutra, Patanjali says that union in action rests on a sturdy tripod of three important elements: willful practice (*tapas*), self–observation (*svadhyaya*), and surrender (*Ishvara-pranidhana*).

Tapas: Will

In classical yoga, tapas refers to both willful practice (also called austerities) and the intense, purifying inner fire that practice produces. From a modern hatha yoga perspective, tapas is primarily the process of getting rid of something undesirable in our systems—from chronic subliminal muscle contraction, to toxicity in our digestive system, to deep-rooted emotions and behaviors. With each of the practices suggested in this book, you and your client are building the strength to burn through old patterns and past conditioning.

Svadhyaya: Self-Study

Practice alone will not support union in action and, in fact, an intense hatha yoga practice without self-study (svadhyaya) might create a rigid armor of self-righteousness or an intense and fiery energy that can be both charismatic and dangerous. Self-study balances the willful practice in this formula. In classical yoga, svadhyaya, or self-study, was the path to deeper self-knowledge. In yoga practice, when we pay attention to the breath and the sensations arising in the body, we are less distracted by the swirl of obsessive thoughts or negative cognitions about ourselves and the world. When I direct my client's attention to the sensations in the palms after a breathing practice that might include a hand gesture called a mudra, I am asking my client to be present in a way that in ordinary life he may not be. "The body is always present," I may say. "The mind is a time traveler." This cue to presence in a session can give the client who suffers from depression or anxiety a momentary glimpse into a calm and steady state of mind, a window into freedom from negative self-talk.

As you cue your client to sense her face, her hands, or her fingertips after leading a yogic breathing exercise or a sound practice, you are teaching her to develop a more observing mind, the witness referred to above. As she learns to do this more often through regular practice, she may cultivate a feeling response to the challenges in her life that is less reactive. Eventually, the witness consciousness on loan from you as her therapist will become her own. This is the goal of svadhyaya.

Svadhyaya or self-study is where yoga practices meet and complement talk therapy, as evidenced by a controlled study funded by the National Institutes of Health. Susan Franzblau and her colleagues at Fayetteville State University in North Carolina examined the effects of pranayama breathing on self-efficacy (Franzblau, Smith, Echevarria, & Van Cantford, 2006). The authors noted that when a woman experiences abuse, the lack of support and loss of self-confidence can result in increased feelings of hopelessness. In this study, both the group that had the opportunity to offer a single session of testimony about the abuse to a trained listener of the same race and the group who was offered a single session of pranayama breathing instruction showed improved self-efficacy as compared to the control group on the waiting list. However, the most significant improvement was measured in the group who participated in both the testimony to a trained listener and pranayama breathing instruction.

Ishvara-Pranidhana: Surrender & Acceptance

With only willful practice and self-study, the first two components of this important sutra, the direction of treatment might take a turn in a harsh, overly analytical, and even self-critical direction. The client may not feel the compassion so necessary to accept what she sees in herself, which of course she must do, if true and lasting change is to occur. It is surrender, the third element of this tripod of active principles, that softens the heart and strengthens it too. Ishvara-pranidhana is usually translated as surrender to the Lord, but, as defined by Patanjali, Ishvara is not a deity in the ordinary sense, but rather the divine in the form of pure awareness—that larger, more spacious awareness, where even the opposites of emotion and belief can be tolerated.

There's another way in which Ishvara-pranidhana can operate in our lives to attenuate suffering. One of the hardest lessons to learn in life is when to let go—of a relationship, a dream, a fantasy, even a mood like fear. Yet once we learn that we can't control people, things, and emotions, when we surrender to and accept reality as it is, we are happier. Sometimes the best therapy is about helping your client accept and make peace with the inconsistencies and losses in her life.

The importance of this kind of surrender was brought home to me when I met a beautiful dance therapist and yoga practitioner, Karen, who taught movement therapy in a university psychology program. At the time, she was moderating a panel on mood and movement at a large health conference, of which I was a member. Karen was the mother of two young sons, and she maintained a daily yoga practice. Less than 3 months before we met, her husband, a pilot, was killed in a much-publicized airplane crash. Though she was in pain over her loss, Karen was not suffering when I met her. She was radiant and calm as she told me about her journey through grief. "I practice," she said, "and I weep. I don't let myself lock down." Karen was facing a number of challenges. As the sole surviving parent, she needed to work full time, even as she raised her young sons with no extended family nearby. But she let grief move through her on her mat, and then rolled it up and got on with her life. In her surrender, she was not in a fight with reality, and so did not escalate the deep pain of her loss into suffering.

Yoga, just like therapy, teaches us that we suffer when our fear of pain and our attempts to avoid it close us off from our potential for growth. For it is from the challenges of life—and we all face them—that we are offered the chance to transform those old karmic patterns that keep us small and separated from the knowledge of who we really are. This is precisely what yoga is meant to teach, not only through our willful practice, but through the cultivation of self-awareness—self-study on and off the mat and through our learning, time after time, to surrender to reality as it is. Through yoga's cultivation of will, self-study, and surrender, we begin to dissolve the armoring that separates us from the knowledge of who we really are.

And Who Are You, Really?

"Who are you really?" is the question the great sages of yoga have asked their students for thousands of years. Yoga affirms the ultimate well-being of each individual. How different therapy might be if instead of seeing the dysfunction, we could see and encourage the client to see that beneath the current mood, the story, and the social mask, there is absolutely nothing wrong? The principles of yoga can help you and your client understand that beneath the diagnostic label, there is a wellspring of wholeness unpolluted by the traumas and losses the client has lived through that is not separate from the ocean of universal wholeness. Einstein rediscovered this. In 1955, he said that we are living in the "optical delusion of our separateness" (Calaprice, 2005, p. 109) and he called this delusion lethal.

Long before Descartian science separated body from mind, the yogis understood that each one of us has everything we need to heal deep within. What this means for you as a clinician is that you are the agent of change for your clients, not by fixing or teaching, but by allowing them moments of seeing that within them, hidden by even the worst abuse and the mental states that arose to cope with that abuse, beneath the most challenging mood disregulation, they can find moments of wholeness and a sense of connection with a nature that is unsullied by their losses and traumas.

The practices in this book can give you strategies to clear a little space through the fog of whatever current mood is present. They can move your client through and beyond any clinging to the old story and his role in it. Joe Walter, the Wisconsin psychotherapist quoted earlier, puts it this way: "It's important to honor the story and, over time, learn to relate differently to the story and, in time, to let go of the story; letting go with a sense of loving kindness. This is where yoga, with its emphasis on tapas, svadhyaha, Isvara pranidhana [will, self-study, and surrender] adds a whole other dimension to the practice of psychotherapy." When yogic principles are integrated into psychotherapy, therapy is "a daily practice grounded in trusting the wholeness of the individual."

PREPARATIONS

As you begin to integrate yoga techniques, you might consider a few guidelines that can help.

Establishing Your Own Practice

Before introducing anything new, you want to feel confident, not only that it works, but in your ability to teach it to your client. The only way to gain this confidence is to practice the yoga tools in this book on your own and to notice the effects on your body and mind. Do what the yogis have done for thousands of years—let your body be your laboratory.

Introducing Yoga in Treatment

Many therapists find that it helps simply to use language that is inviting. "Would you like to try out a new approach that might help calm that revved-up feeling?" might be a good question to ask your client whose speech is rapid upon arrival and who is jumping from thought to thought. Or here's another doorway in: "Perhaps if we begin today's session with a simple breathing exercise, you might find it easier to focus on what is most troubling. Would you like to try that?" Once you have your client's agreement, let her know that she can stop the breathing practice at any time, or interrupt to ask a question if something isn't clear. Let her know that she is in the driver's seat, and you are merely offering her a tool (like a GPS) to get her where she wants to go.

The Safe Container

As a therapist, you already have ways to help your client feel safe and at ease with you in treatment. Perhaps it's the way you greet him with full eye contact and a handshake, your own calm demeanor, or your welcoming smile, along with the promise of confidentiality. I've mentioned how yoga can support the therapeutic bond, establishing a safe and sacred container for your work together from the very first session. The chapters that follow go into more detail about the specific yoga skills you can use in your therapy work, but here I would like to introduce a few general tips that have emerged from my own yoga therapy practice that will help you to create that safe (and sacred) container for the healing work of therapy. These techniques work equally well with groups.

1. Permission: One of the essential elements in a yoga therapy session that can be helpful to therapists as they establish a trusting bond with their clients is the offering of permission. The client has permission to stop whatever guidance has been given or to stop a practice or a process. Letting him know this gives him power over his story and his life.
2. Ritual: A second element that may assist you in cultivating the safe and sacred space for your work together is the repetition of a simple ritual at the beginning of each session, perhaps lighting a candle or leading a centering practice (Figure 2.2).

From my work, I have designed a centering practice for establishing an intention for our work together that I often use with a new client. When leading this or a centering practice of your own design, it helps to speak in a slow, rhythmic, and even tone.

1. Invite your client to close his eyes or, if that doesn't feel comfortable, to simply gaze down at the floor, or at a soothing object in the room.

Figure 2.2. Joy Bennett, LFYP-2, establishing the Safe Container with client

2. Suggest that he sit with his back straight. You might support his spine with a cushion placed between his back and the couch.

3. Cue your client to become aware of his breath: "Without the need to change or do anything different, simply begin to notice the breath moving in and out at the tip of the nostrils."

4. After simply noticing the breath, invite your client to breathe more deeply through the nostrils, filling his lungs with life breath. Invite him to count the beats of his inhalation, and to count the beats of his exhalation.

5. When you see that he is indeed breathing deeply—that his belly is expanding and lifting on the inhalation and gently lowering on the exhalation—invite him to breathe into the spacious, limitless place where he is whole; invite him to breathe beneath the current mood, beneath the social mask. Invite him to breathe into the timeless place where he feels fully, eternally connected to that which is most authentic.

6. And then from this place of wholeness, invite him to allow an intention for the session, an intention that may also have

resonance for his life, to begin to reveal itself to his heart's mind. Allow him to breathe that intention through the clear space he has established with his breathing practice.

7. When he has taken several breaths in this way, invite him to open his eyes, and if he's comfortable, to share his intention with you.

If he hasn't found an intention, then you might probe. What is his current emotional state? And what might be its opposite? Suppose he says he doesn't have an intention, there's just too much chaos in his mind. You might ask him if it would feel comfortable to invite peace to breathe through the chaos—maybe just a small channel to begin. Let him experience this small pathway of peace breathing through the chaos. And then ask him how he feels. You will likely notice a calmer affect and a more focused mind.

Alternatively, you can guide a breathing practice as described above and then guide your client to invite that which she wishes to enhance in her life to surround her heart on the inhalation, and that which blocks the full manifestation of her vision to be released on the exhale.

Finally, you might suggest that she breathe love and acceptance in, and self-judgment out.

What if your client cannot take a deep breath?

1. Meet his shortness of breath with the Stair Step Breath described in Chapter 5.

2. Alternatively, if you and he are comfortable with changing to a lying down position, invite your client into a supine position and ask him to place his hand on his lower abdomen. It is easier to breathe more deeply while lying down, and a hand placed on the belly can help your client not only to direct his breath deeper into his lungs but also to become aware of doing so.

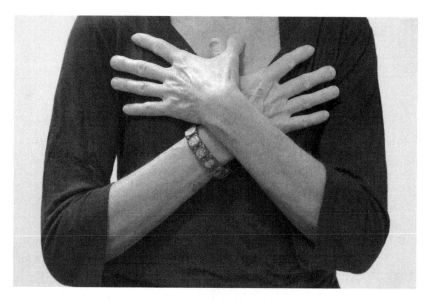

Figure 2.3. Eagle (Garuda) Mudra

Using Gesture (Mudra) & Imagery (Bhavana)

You can create the safe container with gesture. For instance, invite your client to put her right hand on her heart, as though she is pledging allegiance to her heart. This may be enough, or you might suggest that she place her left hand on top, linking her thumbs in a hand gesture called Eagle Mudra (*Garuda*, Figure 2.3).

Add imagery by inviting her to bring into her heart's mind a soothing, serene image, or her inner resource—a place where she can imagine feeling calm and serene. (I avoid using the word *safe*, as the mind, especially in someone who has a history of trauma, may immediately resist—"There is no safe place for me in the world!")

All of these are yogic ways you can adapt to your own way of creating a sense of safety. They may enrich the therapeutic bond and the work you do together in the session.

Other Guidelines

1. While practicing any of these techniques with your client, please remain present with your eyes opened, so that you are fully aware of your client's response to the practice.
2. Let your client know that unless you indicate otherwise for a

particular breath, yogic breathing is done with both inhalation and exhalation through the nostrils, not the mouth.

Some clients, especially those with a history of trauma, may not yet feel safe enough to close the eyes during any of these practices. Normalize your client's wish to keep her eyes opened by suggesting that she may do so before you begin. Guide her to a soft focused gaze with eyes toward the floor or suggest that she gaze at a soothing object in the room.

YOGA MEETS TRAUMA—WHAT STYLE OF YOGA SHOULD YOU RECOMMEND?

If someone is in an acute stage of PTSD, what kind of class would be best? Keeping in mind the general principles covered above, *slow* is the guiding word for working on the yoga mat with someone suffering from PTSD. Likely the trauma, sexual or otherwise, has left a residue or constriction in the physical body. For those who have been sexually traumatized, it may not feel safe to live in the body. Such clients have often developed protective parts that keep them living from the neck up. Yoga can be a gentle way for your client to reclaim her body. That's why body awareness, body-scanning exercises, and body-sensing yoga, where movement is accompanied by mindful attention to sensation and breath, are vital core practices for those suffering from PTSD. Living in the body again can be scary, and yoga is a safe way to begin to make healing connections between mind and body.

A First Step
Body-sensing yoga, a good first step for someone who is suffering from PTSD, includes slow, meditative movement with an emphasis on grounding. Throughout a class, the practitioner is cued to notice body sensations. An effective strategy is to guide the student to the areas in the body where there are a lot of nerve endings, such as the lips, fingers, palms, feet, or whatever part of the body has been

engaged in the preceding yoga movement. In body-sensing yoga there is nothing to achieve. Aside from attending to basic safety issues, there is no right or wrong way to do the pose. The practitioner is encouraged to feel that there is no way to get it wrong. He has total permission to modify and adapt. If body-sensing yoga is a group experience, the students may exhibit many different interpretations of the teacher's guidance. The teacher encourages a deep inquiry into sensation throughout the practice, which encourages the student to remain present and at home in her body. This window into the body-centered moment facilitates a "reoccupation" of the body as a safe place. Senior teachers of this style of yoga practice as developed by the nondual teacher Jean Klein are psychologist Richard Miller and, in Canada, Joan Ruvinsky. (Nondual means "not two," and implies a view of the world in which there is no separation. Despite appearances of distinctions among objects, there is an ultimate knowing that all is one. This ancient view correlates with modern physics.)

There are now specialty "trauma sensitive" yoga classes and styles of yoga practice like Mindfulness Yoga, LifeForce Yoga, and Kripalu Yoga that emphasize body-sensing. Even alignment-based styles of yoga can be adapted to a body-sensing approach by cueing students to direct sensation, and many good teachers in various yoga schools already teach this way.

Clinical social worker Sherry Rubin has both yoga therapy and a 30-year psychotherapy practice outside Philadelphia. When 34-year-old Linda came to her office, her history of trauma and loss was so severe that talking triggered her. She had been sexually molested by a grandparent when she was 7 and raped at 14. When she was 17, her boyfriend was killed in an automobile accident returning home after she told him he couldn't spend the night. Linda blames herself. She is raising one daughter as a single parent and gave another up for adoption, a loss she still grieves. Her first visit occurred shortly after the death of her older sister, whom she had been caring for through her final months of cancer.

But Linda was in treatment for a long time before Sherry learned any of this. At their first meeting, Linda could barely mention the recent death of her sister. As Linda tried to talk about her history during subsequent sessions, Sherry observed that her breathing was shallow, that she was holding her breath, and that her agitation peaked in panic episodes. "Regardless of my approach," said Sherry, "I was triggering PTSD symptoms." Sherry came to appreciate later that Linda's panic and PTSD were triggered by the combination of being in the office, her fearful thoughts, and the belief that she had to talk to heal. "I could readily see that her nervous system needed calming, and that until she was able to learn when to approach the loaded material, when to leave it alone, and most importantly, how to soothe herself, that we would be in an endless loop of retraumatization. Although I offered approaches such as EMDR and EFT, their mere mention made her nervous. She was surprised and then relieved when I told her that all trauma didn't need to be 'talked about' to heal. I let her know that until she could learn how to regulate her nervous system, talking about her trauma would be counterproductive."

Sherry began slowly with the breath, first increasing the exhale to match the inhale, then extending the exhale. Next she helped Linda create an inner sanctuary by using imagery (bhavana), guiding her to a place that for her was peaceful, beautiful, and soothing. Although this was helpful, Sherry observed that the office session was more challenging than restorative. "Because I knew she went for walks and tried to spend as much time outside in nature as possible, I suggested a large local lake surrounded by trees. This became known as my 'lake office.'"

At the park, Sherry taught Linda mountain pose (tadasana), a simple standing posture that many therapists use in the office to help their clients ground. Sherry led the pose, inch by inch, starting with instructions for "finding her feet," making the connection with ground, Mother Earth, and feeling the support and the energy flowing through her. "With the support of the water and trees, a container large enough to hold all the pain she had experienced,

Linda began to use her words occasionally without being triggered, and her history emerged." Sherry guided her to find her intention (*sankalpa*) and a vision for her life, and once she identified these, suggested they become the compass by which Linda could make choices. As she was being drawn toward destructive behaviors or hurtful people, she could ask herself, "Will this bring me closer, keep me here, or take me further away from what I want to manifest in my life?"

Sherry said, "Linda pushes herself and always works hard, but she is learning how to trust that tuning into and listening to her body with simple yoga techniques will guide her home to her whole, healed self. Together we are both learning how much less is more."

A Possible Second Step

When a level of trust has been established between teacher and student, yoga can be used therapeutically in a different way. Long holds as mentioned in Chapter 1, for example, within the safety of a class or an individual session with a qualified yoga teacher or therapist, are a way to begin to release the trauma and loss stored in the body. Long holding of a pose would not be the first intervention, and it is not recommended with a group or an individual with acute PTSD, unless the student has been adequately prepared and a mental health professional who is experienced in trauma treatment is present.

Holding a pose for an extended period of time may facilitate a deep release of tension and the residue of trauma stored in the body. This experience is not about the "story." Rather, it's about a release from the physical, emotional, and mental bodies, with no story attached. It is therefore important that the facilitator coach participants to neither get caught up in words or analysis, nor to numb out, but rather to stay present to the sensations in the body. A therapeutic long holding is an opportunity to release old patterns from the physical body, particularly those held at the core—the hips and the psoas muscle. The psoas is the only muscle that runs both front and back and above and below the waist. When we are startled, this muscle often tightens. When there has been chronic trauma, there can be a pattern of physical constriction in this area of the body, affecting the diaphragm, hips, pelvis, and even the reproductive organs. Even if no emotion is felt, the actual trembling that occurs in this area will likely jar loose some of the tension held at the core.

THE GOAL

Finally, when we make use of yoga skills in psychotherapy or yoga therapy, we are not there to fix problems but to welcome and accept and then to educate. We offer our clients and students the timeless tools of yoga to clear the obstructions that keep them from realizing their wholeness—the truth of their own true nature, which is always complete, always safe. When you integrate yoga-based skills into your therapy practice, you are educating those who suffer. Not only are you offering your clients strategies for self-care that will last a lifetime but, equally important, you are reminding them of who they really are by providing tools to clear away the obstacles to their own felt sense of wholeness.

With these basic guidelines and preparations in place, you're ready to incorporate more yoga skills into your practice. Let's begin by exploring the yoga of breath—pranayama—in more detail.

CHAPTER 3 CLEARING THE SPACE: THE YOGA OF BREATH (Pranayama)

According to Robert Provine at the University of Maryland, unlike chimps, our closest species relatives, we humans have voluntary control over our breath, likely because we walk upright (Pease, 2004). Control of the breath not only enables language but gives us a measure of control over our mood. *Pranayama* means the "control of life breath" or "life force." Teaching pranayama breathing exercises to your client is like teaching a teenager when to accelerate and when to brake the car. The ancient yogis understood that when you consciously regulate the breath, you can manage your feelings and moods by accelerating your energy or by putting on the brakes. Harnessing *prana* (life force) through pranayama breathing exercises will increase your client's feelings of self-efficacy and control. Certain breathing practices will give your client a feeling of power at the solar plexus. It's like revving the engine, moving from 6 horsepower to 60.

WHY WORK WITH THE BREATH?

If you could learn a simple, 10-second breathing exercise that could shift your energy between clients, one that you can then teach your clients so they too can create a paradigm mood shift, would that be helpful? I invite you to try this with me right now. This Smile Breath is easy enough that you can read the following instructions and then close your eyes to practice. Or, if you prefer, keep your eyes open and practice as you read. You can sit in whatever position you happen to be reading in now, as long as your spine is straight. Take a deep inhale through the nostrils, hold the breath for a heart-beat or two, and then during the length of your exhale, drop your chin to your chest. Hold the breath out for a heartbeat or two, as you lift the corners of your mouth. Inhale and lift your head. Exhale and open your eyes. How do you feel? If you're like me and my students and clients, you likely feel calmer.

So what elements of the Smile Breath might affect your mood? First of all, to practice this simple breath, you need to pause for a moment, taking a break from the thoughts and feelings rolling through your mind. Second, taking just one deep breath uses more of your lungs than you may have been using the moment before. In that instant, you are bringing more oxygen into your system, feed-ing your brain. Think about the slumped shoulders and shallow breath that often accompanies depression. Think about the short shallow breath that often accompanies anxiety. In both anxiety and depression, there is often not enough oxygen in the blood flow-ing to the brain. Taking a deep breath can begin to reverse that. Third, when you lift the corners of your mouth, you are likely lift-ing the mood. A 2006 small-scale pilot trial, published in the *Journal of Dermatologic Surgery*, found that Botox injected into frown lines around the mouth or in forehead furrows of 10 women eliminated depression symptoms in 9 of them and reduced symptoms in the 10th (Finzi & Wasserman, 2006).

Previous research has shown that the 12-step adage, "fake it until you make it," may have some validity. More than 20 years ago, researchers at Loma Linda University School of Medicine showed the biochemical changes produced by laughter—reductions in serum levels of cortisol, dopac, and epinephrine (Berk et al., 1989).

Since then, a number of studies have looked at the efficacy of laughter and smiling in improving self-efficacy in the workplace, mood in cancer patients, depression in the elderly, and preoperative effects on children undergoing surgery (Ko & Youn, 2011; Mora-Ripoll, 2010; Noji & Takayanagi, 2010; Shahidi et al., 2011). In all cases reviewed, laughing "for no reason" has had a positive effect on mood. The body doesn't know the difference. Your dopamine level is going to increase and other feel-good chemicals are likely to elevate whether you are smiling "for the camera" or for real. Not only can a smile be invited into a simple breathing practice as above, but many of the mood-elevating pranayama breathing practices I explore in Chapter 4 and the sound practices in Chapter 5 physically duplicate a good belly laugh.

In a 2009 article published in the *Annals of the New York Academy of Sciences*, Drs. Patricia Gerbarg and Richard Brown reviewed a number of studies that cite evidence that yogic breath work may be efficacious for the treatment of depression, anxiety, and post-traumatic stress disorder, and for victims of mass disasters. "By inducing stress resilience," said the authors, "breath work enables us to rapidly and compassionately relieve many forms of suffering." For most of the evidence, the authors examined the extensive studies that have been done on the breathing practices taught by the Art of Living Foundation, which include three-stage slow resistance breathing (*Ujjayi* or Victory Breath), Bellows Breath (*Bhastrika*), chanting "Om," and *Sudarshan Kriya* (cyclical breathing). However, by extrapolating from the common elements within the variety of breathing practices taught in Tibetan and yogic tradition, along with those taught by the Art of Living, the authors were able to suggest that "the separate and combined effects of yoga practices enrich our understanding of the impact of yoga practices on the self-repair and self-regulatory systems that may increase longevity, resilience, and quality of life" (Brown & Gerbarg, 2009 p. 56)

HOW WE BREATHE

The actual process of respiration takes place within the cells of the body. Not only are your nose, trachea (windpipe), and lungs involved, but the process of transporting oxygen from the air and modifying it to make it available to your cells also involves your circulatory system and the muscles in your chest. Mechanically, we draw oxygen into the lungs in two ways. We can extend the diaphragm down, which feels like a deep breath into the belly. This is diaphragmatic breathing, and it is the most efficient means of exposing the blood in the capillaries to air. It also circulates oxygenated blood to the lower, gravity-dependent parts of the lungs. This is the way a newborn breathes and it is the most efficient way to breathe in our normal, daily activities.

Unfortunately, most of us have forgotten how to breathe this way. Instead we most often use thoracic breathing, which is breathing into the upper chest. This breath expands the ribcage, using the intercostals, the muscles located between the ribs. Chest breathing is not as efficient as diaphragmatic breathing, because the lower portions of the lungs are not exposed to air. To get the same amount of oxygen to the cells, chest breathing requires a lot more work than diaphragmatic breathing, and it is ultimately more work for the heart.

MEETING THE MOOD WITH THE BREATH

When clinical psychologist Deborah Lubetkin began working with Barbara, a middle-aged female who had been in therapy on and off since the age of 13, Barbara reported that her anxiety and obsessive thoughts were the greatest they had been in a long time, and she felt out of control. "She had been on Prozac for many years," says Deborah, "and she felt it had stopped working. She could not get comfortable." Barbara was so anxious at the beginning of treatment that in the first session, Deborah started with a balancing breath that both calms and energizes. She introduced a triangular 4:4:4 count breath. The first side of the triangle is a four-count inhalation. The next side is a four-count retention of the breath. The third side is a four-count exhalation. The short retention after the inhalation is lightly energizing. The even count is balancing. The count is relatively short and easy for most people to accomplish. In making the choice to begin with this breath, Deborah was meeting Barbara's anxiety and bringing it into balance. Had Deborah instead chosen a calming breath, it might not have worked. Because Barbara was revved up, she might have struggled and failed to extend the breath longer on exhalation than on inhalation, which is a breathing pattern known to be more calming. This failure, right in the first session, could have reinforced her level of discomfort and her lack of self-esteem and may even have damaged the developing therapeutic alliance.

By the same token, if someone is suffering from major depression, she might not be able to muster the energy and motivation it takes to breathe rapidly and forcefully, two elements common to several breathing practices useful in treating depression covered in Chapter 4. Instead, you might meet her depressed mood with a slower breath, gradually deepening and picking up the pace.

Ann Friedenheim, a psychotherapist and yoga teacher who specializes in addictions, took just this approach with Lenore, who was referred to outpatient treatment as part of her probation requirement following a 2-year prison stay. "She was not very happy about being in counseling again," Ann said, "and was feeling quite angry about the controls placed on her by the criminal justice system." In addition, Lenore was unable to find work, partly the result of the felonies on her record. These circumstances, combined with being separated from her children, manifested as what had been diagnosed by a local psychiatrist as major depression. Lenore, who had once been a heroin addict, was not open to taking medication and struggled with her symptoms. She agreed with Ann on a treatment plan that included yoga.

Lenore often came into sessions feeling lethargic, irritable, and unwilling to talk. Since Lenore was open to trying another approach besides talking, she was willing to follow Ann's suggestion to begin in a supine position on the floor, where she was guided to follow her breath and was introduced to Yogic Three-Part Breath (*Dirga Pranayama*; Figure 3.1). Dirga is a slow, deep, diaphragmatic breath covered in the next chapter. Since Lenore was lying down and breathing slowly, this choice of breath clearly met her lethargic mood. Ann then began to pick up the pace by introducing Sun

Figure 3.1. Ann Friedenheim, MA, leading Yogic Three-Part Breath with a client

Breaths on the floor, which includes inhaling and raising the arms over the head and exhaling and lowering them to the sides. Ann drew Lenore's attention to the way she could control her breath and make the inhale and exhale coordinate with the movement of the arms. This cuing can increase the client's sense of self-efficacy and control.

Next, she asked Lenore to sit up and practice Stair Step Breath, which is even more energizing. I cover this breath in Chapter 5. After 15–20 minutes of gentle moving and breath work, Ann said that Lenore felt she could focus and was willing to engage in the therapy session.

INTRODUCING YOGA BREATHING TO YOUR CLIENT

Therapists can be reluctant to introduce their clients to a breathing practice for many reasons. It may seem too New Age or esoteric. The therapist may be unsure of the specific technique and its likely effect. Or she may just not have the words to introduce and explain it properly. I highly recommend that therapists practice the breath for 40 days before attempting to teach it to a client. You will yourself then experience the variations in the practice and their effects on your state of mind. Use this book as a guide for your own practice. If you prefer a guided practice, CDs, audio downloads, and DVDs are listed in the resource section in Chapter 10 that can walk you and your clients through each of the strategies recommended in this book. If you practice with one of them regularly, you will feel confident in using simple language to teach the technique to your client.

One way to warm your client to the idea of beginning a breathing practice is to mention the research. Some therapists like to download a study from the Internet like those quoted above, and then they provide their clients with a handout citing the efficacy of yogic breathing, along with guidance for finding practice tools like the resources covered in Chapter 10. This book may also be a useful tool for your client's direct use.

So how did Ann Friedenheim convince her reluctant client Lenore, unfamiliar with yoga, to begin her session by lying on the floor and paying attention to her breath? "I explained to her that yoga could be approached from many levels. I explained that she could consider it a physical practice for health, flexibility, and overall well-being," Ann said.

WEAVING IN LESSONS FOR THE CLIENT

During and following breathing practices, it is easy to offer supportive messages that buttress your and your client's goals for treatment, whether toward greater self-acceptance, greater self-awareness, a sense of belonging, or the need for change.

Ann introduced ideas that would support Lenore's recovery as they were working with the breath, such as learning to know when to control and when to let go. As Ann led Lenore through breathing practices, guiding her to observe the breath at the outset of the session, she used words that helped Lenore understand that as she learned to observe her breath and the sensations in her body during gentle movement, she was also learning to live with discomfort without reacting. As Lenore moved into a pleasant and calmer mind state, during and following the breathing practice, Ann pointed out that in doing so, she was developing self-acceptance and contentment with what is ("learning to live life on life's terms"). During the course of her therapy with Ann, one of the most important lessons for Lenore, who was slowly piecing together a healthier life for herself that would include the return of her children, was learning to be patient with processes that take time. Ann's reminders of what she was gaining in her breathing practice helped her do that.

GETTING STARTED

It's fine for most clients to learn these breathing exercises in a seated position. Simply give them the instruction to sit upright with both feet planted firmly on the floor. You might suggest a cushion behind the back as a way of supporting a straight spine. Now that we are talking about calming breaths, it bears repeating that unless you indicate otherwise, yoga breathing is done with both inhalation and exhalation through the nostrils, not the mouth. This style of breathing is more stimulating to the parasympathetic nervous system and therefore more relaxing.

For someone who finds deep breathing difficult, you might, as Ann Friedenheim did with her client Lenore, invite her to take a supine position on the floor. Learning to breathe deeply is easier when the spine is fully extended and the lungs are not compressed in a slumped seated position.

REMAINING PRESENT

How fortunate you are that as you teach your client a breathing practice, you can practice too. But as I mentioned in Chapter 1 pertaining to all yoga practices, it is especially important when guiding your client in a breathing exercise that you practice with your eyes open so that you are immediately aware if your client is struggling. By staying alert in an eyes-open position, you can offer a modification or a different breath. There's another good reason to keep your own eyes open. When some people who have been shallow breathers for most of their lives begin to breathe deeply, emotion can arise unexpectedly. Even if you have prepared your client by telling her that feelings may arise during breathing practice, if tears come for no apparent reason and unexpectedly, fear and shame may accompany them. Acknowledging and even honoring tears is an important aspect of setting the safe container.

I worked with a client who had once maintained a twice-weekly power yoga practice at a gym but, because of her husband's job, she had recently moved from London to Tucson and had not practiced regularly in 2 years. Sally felt alone, since her 6-year-old was in school all day for the first time and her husband often traveled on business. They had moved to an upscale neighborhood where she felt she didn't belong, and she had not yet made friends. Though she did not have a clinical diagnosis, she said she had gained weight, felt lethargic, and, except for bouts of irritability, she felt numb. Since her previous yoga experience did not focus on the breath, after setting the safe container during our first session, I suggested that she begin in a supine position, lying on her back. I supported her with a bolster under her back so that her chest was open and breathing was easier. I also placed a thin folded blanket beneath her head to tuck the chin forward slightly, which supports the mind to relax. Within a couple of minutes of deep, diaphragmatic breathing, she was sobbing. There was an immediate connection to the loneliness and anger she had felt as a young child, when her father died and her mother, overcome with grief, had not been emotionally available.

I brought her into a sitting position, so that she could breathe and then eventually to her feet, where we could more easily begin to move the emotion that had been triggered through her body. As she left, her eyes were shining and her face was serene, and she had a referral to two psychotherapists in our community.

There are three important lessons here. First, the importance of establishing the safe container, which not only gives the client permission to "put on the brakes," as Babette Rothschild (2003) says in *The Body Remembers*, but also includes a normalization of the tears that can arise. One way I do this is to quote Swami Kripalu— "Crying is one of the highest spiritual practices. One who knows crying, knows yoga" (Weintraub, 2004).

The second lesson is about staying present with your client throughout the practices you lead, and that means your own eyes are open and you are monitoring her experience at all times.

The third lesson is how complementary yoga and psychotherapy actually are. When Sally began working with her body and her breath, she opened to a deeper sadness. She was finally ready to seek out talk therapy along with her return to the yoga mat, something that her current situation, as miserable as it was, had not motivated her to do.

In conclusion, as you integrate yoga breathing into your work with clients, you are not only empowering them by offering a tool to help them regulate their emotions, you are enhancing your own wellbeing.

COOLING THE BREATH, CALMING THE MIND: BREATHING PRACTICES FOR ANXIETY

We can all benefit from the self-soothing breathing practices you will find in this chapter. The first two practices are a wonderful way to begin a session to help your client focus and relax. However, if the client presents with a highly anxious mood, you might want to start with one of the energizing practices in Chapter 4. That way you can meet her anxiety and then, as Deborah Lubetkin described in Chapter 2, you can introduce a more calming breath to guide your client back into a balanced state of mind.

In the practices outlined below, I have suggested a 4:4 count, which means inhaling for four beats and exhaling for four. This count is manageable for most people and a good place to start. However, the calming effect will be enhanced if the exhalation is lengthened so that it is twice as long as the inhalation. Once you and your clients are comfortable with 4:4, for maximum benefit, extend the exhalation to six or even eight counts, so that the ratio of inhalation to exhalation is 1:2.

YOGIC THREE-PART BREATH (Dirga Pranayama)

Yogic Three-Part Breath creates a state of mental alertness, even as it activates the parasympathetic nervous system so that the body-mind is calm. Long extension of the exhalation enhances the calming effect. The ideal ratio for calming and cooling is 1:2, although for teaching purposes, begin this breath with a 1:1 ratio.

There are two methods of practicing Yogic Three-Part Breath. In the traditional method, taught in most lineages, the inhalation is directed to the bottom of the lungs, the midsection, and then the top. The exhalation moves from top to bottom. In some yoga traditions, like Krishnamacharya, the breath is drawn in and then exhaled in exactly the opposite direction. From a psychophysical perspective both methods have the same effect. I practice and teach the more traditional method. However, if you have been taught and practice the method favored by the lineages that extend from Krishnamacharya, please feel free to continue to practice and teach Yogic Three-Part Breath that way. Remember that both the inhalation and the exhalation are done through the nose.

1. Begin in a comfortable seated position with the spine erect. Inhale the breath through the nose into the bottom of the lungs so the belly expands. It can help to place the right hand on the abdomen so the extension can be easily felt. Practice this first part at least three times or until the breath is smooth and you can see your client's abdomen rising with the inhalation and falling with the exhalation.
2. Inhale the first third of the breath into the bottom of the lungs as above, and then inhale the second third into the midsection of the lungs so that the ribcage expands. Practice this three times or until there is a sense of ease with the breath.
3. Place the left hand on your upper chest, and inhale as above with the final third of the breath moving up into the top of the lungs, and feel your upper chest lift.

Figure 4.1. Amy Weintraub demonstrating the use of props to facilitate Yogic Three-Part Breath with LifeForce Yoga® Practitioner and yoga teacher, Kat Larsen

4. Slowly release the breath and feel the upper chest lowering first. As you complete the exhale, draw your abdomen up and back toward your spine, completely emptying the bottom of your lungs.
5. To begin, practice Yogic Three-Part Breath for 3 to 5 minutes.

Modifications

If the breath is constricted and your client has trouble breathing deeply, you can invite him to lie down. It is easier to breathe into the bottom of the lung and extend the abdomen while lying in a supine position. You can further open up the chest, increasing lung capacity, by using a prop like a low bolster or folded blanket, as shown in Figure 4.1.

Application

Yogic Three-Part Breath can be a wonderful way to begin a therapy session with any clients, as it will help them to shake off any anxiety they may bring in with them. Following a 3- to 5-minute practice, your client will likely feel more centered and focused and have greater access to his feelings. You can enhance the practice of this breath by combining it with Ocean-Sounding Victory Breath, described below. You can practice both breaths seated or in a supine position.

Laura Orth, a psychotherapist in the Boston area, was working with an 8-year-old girl in treatment for severe anxiety. Heidi became nauseated and vomited in unfamiliar situations. After extensive inquiry, Laura determined that she did not have a history of trauma. Heidi was referred by her pediatrician when she began to lose weight. Laura tried several cognitive approaches for anxiety containment, but despite diligent practice and support from her mother, the anxiety continued. When Laura introduced Yogic Three-Part Breath in session, Heidi began to respond to treatment. Laura began by inviting Heidi to lie down and put her hands on her belly so she could feel her breath move. "This task gave her a focus," said Laura, "and that was helpful in redirecting her energy and emotions." After learning the breath along with Heidi, her mother prompted regular practice at home. Over several months of practice, Heidi's anxiety improved. "Now when I see her, Heidi proudly tells me how many months have gone by without vomiting. I notice after practicing in session that her rate of speech is slower, her body movements are more fluid, and she is less vigilant of her environment."

OCEAN-SOUNDING VICTORY BREATH (Ujjayi)

This breath, jokingly referred to as Darth Vader Breath, is soothing to the central nervous system, even as it calms the mind and supports greater focus.

1. To begin, invite your client to inhale through the nostrils with a slight constriction at the back of the throat, so that the breath is audible, like a light snoring sound.

2. The exhalation is also through the nostrils, maintaining the snoring sound.

3. The breath is slow, and Yogic Three-Part Breath may be included by suggesting that your client feel the breath expanding the belly, the ribcage, and then the upper chest.

4. On the exhalation, pull the abdomen in and up to empty the lungs completely.

    Additional Suggestions:

1. Inquire if the breath is felt at the back of the throat. This kind of cueing heightens body awareness, often lacking in clients who have been traumatized and for whom it no longer feels safe to live in a body.

2. Imagery: You might suggest that the sound is like a wave gently rolling across pebbles, and invite your client to imagine her favorite pebbly beach.

3. You can offer warm associations for the client. For example, you might suggest that the sound is like a baby's snore.

4. If your client is working on nurturing very young parts of himself, you can say that the breath is like a lullaby to himself or to the 6-year-old in his heart.

5. Combined with a hand on the heart or an image of holding the part of the client that may need acceptance or love or compassion, this breath can be a powerful tool for self-soothing.

Modifications

Most clients will learn this breath easily. For those who are struggling to make the sound, you can begin with an invitation to breathe in and out through the mouth, as though fogging a mirror. You can suggest that your client bring her hand a few inches in front of her mouth, simulating the mirror. Have your client take several breaths in this manner. Once she has mastered the slow steady rhythmic breath with the sound, invite her to close her mouth and practice the same breathing through the nostrils.

Application

Ocean-Sounding Victory Breath may be combined with Yogic Three-Part Breath to enhance the calming effects of both breaths.

Ocean-Sounding Victory Breath was one of several breathing strategies that Sue Tebb, PhD, yoga teacher and professor of social work at the University of St. Louis, taught to a Bosnian women's group once a week for 5 months. The women, who had been victims of torture, were encouraged to practice at home, finding a time and place that would allow them to focus on themselves and the breathing and postures. Sue said, "In the sessions, I discussed strategies to incorporate the techniques into daily activities as they began to experience symptoms of stress, such as when driving, waiting in the line at the grocery store, or working with the immigration office."

Sue was working with an interpreter and was initially unsure whether they were practicing at home. One day, while in a session, the tornado sirens went off and the group retreated to the dark dank basement, where Sue continued her LifeForce Yoga class until the warnings stopped. The next week several women reported that they realized how yoga was affecting them in positive ways. "In previous tornado warnings, they were frightened and very anxious," said Sue. "This time they were not triggered into experiencing the negative symptoms; instead they realized they controlled their feelings through the yogic techniques."

The women continued to describe ways they were using the yoga techniques in their lives. Sue said, "One woman reported yogic breathing helped her to focus only on her breath, and it prevented her from thinking about all the past events that triggered emotional and physical pain, such as the loss of a child and not being able to return to Bosnia. The group realized together that a safe space had been created in the sessions where feelings could be expressed and techniques were readily accessible to them that could be used when needed in other triggered environments to lessen depression and anxiety."

ALTERNATE-NOSTRIL PURIFYING BREATH (Nadi Shodhana)

The ancient yogis believed that there were 72,000 tubelike channels through the body called *nadis*. Some contemporary yoga practitioners correlate the nadis to the nerves, while others think of the network of nadis in purely spiritual terms. Either way, from a yogic perspective, it is important to keep as many nadis open as possible, so that the maximum prana (life force, energy, breath) may be conducted through the body. Scientific research is corroborating what the yogis understood in ancient times—that alternate-nostril breathing balances the left and right hemispheres of the brain (Telles, Nagaratha, & Nagendra, 1994).

1. Sit with the spine erect. Use a hand gesture called *Vishnu Mudra* by making a fist of your right hand. Next, release the thumb and the third and fourth fingers, leaving the index and middle fingers folded against your palm (Figure 4.2).
2. Place the thumb against your right nostril and slowly inhale through the left nostril for the count of four (about 6 seconds).
3. Close off the left nostril with the third and fourth finger of your right hand. Then release your thumb and slowly exhale through your right nostril for the count of four.
4. Inhale through your right nostril for the count of four, and then close off the right nostril.
5. Lift your fourth and fifth fingers and exhale through your left nostril for the count of four.
6. Repeat the sequence on both sides for three more rounds, ending with an exhalation through the left nostril.

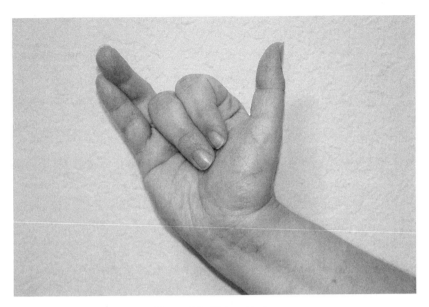

Figure 4.2. Vishnu Mudra

Keep the inhalation even with the exhalation. Guide your client through three to five rounds to begin. So that he has the integrating experience of guiding himself, allow him to practice on his own for two rounds. You might say, "Practice two more rounds, ending by exhaling through your left nostril." By ending with the left nostril, you are favoring the right hemisphere and helping your client establish a calm and centered state of mind.

Upon completion, suggest that your client sit with eyes closed and notice how he is feeling. With the eyes remaining closed, ask him to notice if he is feeling calmer, more focused, more alert. Pause between each suggested state of mind, so that he has a chance to absorb and reflect on what you are asking. When he opens his eyes, check in with him, asking him to describe his experience and what he is feeling now.

Modifications

You or your client may find that one nostril is blocked. To a certain extent, it is normal for one nostril to be more open, or dominant, than the other. Nostril dominance shifts on an average of every 2 hours, but the actual range varies among individuals from 25 minutes to 4 hours. For most of us, our nostrils are more balanced at dawn and dusk, which is one reason the yogis have traditionally practiced yoga and meditation at these times. But some of us who have had injuries, surgery, a deviated septum, or a range of other conditions have a pattern of right or left nostril predominance, which can show up in the size of our nostrils.

As part of my assessment of a new client, I not only ask about breathing problems, nasal surgeries, and injuries, but I actually look at my client's nostrils. If the right nostril is slightly enlarged and he tells me that he primarily breathes through that nostril because his left nostril is occluded, it may indicate a lifelong tendency toward anxiety, indicative of left hemispheric dominance. Right nostril/left hemisphere dominance may also indicate a strong sense of order and linear thinking—a wonderful attribute for surgeons, pilots, and flight controllers. Take that orderliness and organization too far, and it might begin to look like obsessive-compulsive disorder or other highly anxious states of mind.

If you or your clients have trouble inhaling and exhaling through

Figure 4.4. Mechanically opening the left nasal passage

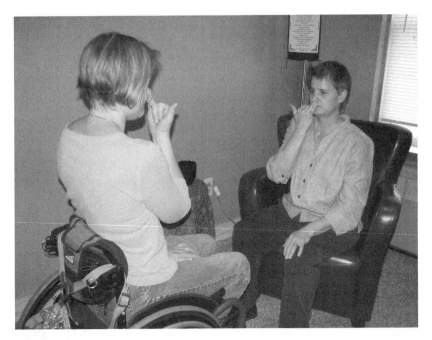

Figure 4.4. Sue Dilsworth, PhD, introducing
Alternate Nostril Purifying Breath to a client

the left nostril while practicing Alternate-Nostril Purifying Breath, you can open the nasal passage by using the left hand to stretch the skin of the left cheek toward the left ear (Figure 4.3). On the other hand, if the right nostril is constricted, continue using the right hand for alternating airflow between the right and left nostrils, and cross the left hand beneath the right and stretch the skin of the right cheek toward the right ear.

Alternatively, you can press the ring finger of the right hand at the base and to the left of the left nostril to free more space through that nasal passage. You can press the thumb at the base and to the right of the right nostril to free more space through that nasal passage.

Application
Alternate-Nostril Purifying Breath is one of the primary breathing practices in the yogic tradition, and it has many applications for you and your clients (Figure 4.4). Practice this breath as a way to center yourself before you see your clients, between clients, and with your clients. You will feel calm and yet alert, ready to meet

your client in a responsive, compassionate, and clear-minded way. You can practice this breath before meditation or any time you would like to enhance feelings of equanimity.

I worked with a client who had practiced yoga as a form of exercise, without attention to the breath. Pam worked in a male-dominated field as a bridge engineer in the public sector, and in fact was the senior member of a team of engineers, all men. She often felt under scrutiny, as though her colleagues would pounce if she made a mistake. She felt she had become perfectionistic, highly critical of herself and others, and hypervigilant about suspected slights. Because she was practicing in a driven, perfectionistic way, even yoga wasn't helping her relax, and she often left a yoga class feeling more tense and self-judging than when she arrived. When I introduced yoga breathing, she was at first concerned that it would take time away from the little time she had to practice her postures and slow down her vigorous practice, and therefore, she reasoned, the physiological benefits of her morning routine would be reduced. Learning Alternate-Nostril Purifying Breath did indeed slow down Pam's practice, for which she eventually felt grateful. She felt it also balanced her perfectionistic tendencies and reported that she was less critical. Not only did she incorporate the breathing into her morning routine, but she also used it at work. When she noticed anxious, judging, or defensive feelings arising, she would take a bathroom break and practice a few rounds of alternate-nostril breathing. She returned to her work, be it a meeting or a design project at her desk, feeling relaxed and clear and more creative.

Michigan psychologist Sue Dilsworth uses Alternate-Nostril Purifying Breath in her clinical practice along with other pranayamas. "These techniques can be taught in an office setting," she says, "and can be practiced efficiently anywhere." With an anxious client who was back in school after losing his job as an airline pilot, the breath was "a useful and helpful technique for him in terms of establishing a sense of calm."

Felicity Boyer, a LifeForce Yoga Practitioner in northern Virginia, often teaches Alternate-Nostril Purifying Breath as one of the first forms of pranayama because she feels it's easy to use and highly effective in reducing anxiety in a wide variety of people and situations. One of her students used it in a corporate setting to help her prepare for a meeting that she anticipated would be confrontational. When she realized she was becoming increasingly anxious before the meeting, she shut her office door and did several rounds of Alternate-Nostril Purifying Breath to bring her back into emotional balance. When she was done, she felt calm and composed. She went to the meeting and handled the situation calmly and professionally. She gave credit for her poise to the breathing technique, which helped her calm herself quickly and privately. She told Felicity that she is now a big believer in the power of breath to help calm her anxiety.

LEFT NOSTRIL BREATHING (Chandra Bheda)

Left Nostril Breathing is a way to slow down, activating the right hemisphere of the brain and the parasympathetic nervous system. Many clients may find it helps them calm down before sleep. It may be useful in the treatment of insomnia. Shirley Telles, PhD, a research psychologist and the leading researcher in the field of yoga therapy, coauthored an early study on the effects of unilateral breathing that clearly demonstrates the stimulation of the parasympathetic nervous system with the practice of Left Nostril Breathing (Telles et al., 1994).

The safest, easiest way to practice this form of unilateral breathing is to breathe slowly in through the left nostril and slowly out through the right, regulating the airflow between nostrils with the right-hand fingers in the hand gesture described above (Vishnu Mudra; Figure 4.5).

1. Begin with the right thumb closing the right nostril.
2. Inhale through the left nostril to the count of four and then

Figure 4.5. Left Nostril Breathing with Vishnu Mudra

cover the left nostril with the fourth and fifth fingers of the right hand and exhale for the count of four through the right nostril.

3. Repeat this pattern up to 20 times. When working with insomnia, extend the exhalation longer (six or eight counts) than the inhalation.

There are variations of unilateral breathing that keep the breath moving through the left nostril for both inhalation and exhalation. The effect is stronger, so if practicing Left Nostril Breathing in this way, be sure to conclude with a few rounds of Alternate-Nostril Purifying Breath.

Modifications

As in the practices previously discussed, you can extend the exhalation to enhance the effect of Left Nostril Breathing. If the nasal passage is constricted, you can open it with the left hand with one of the two methods described above in Alternate-Nostril Purifying Breath.

Contraindications

You would not want to practice Left Nostril Breathing for an extended period of time if you or your client suffers from depressed mood, as it can magnify the lethargy that often accompanies depression.

Application

In my work with a postmenopausal woman whose sleep had been disrupted for years, I suggested that she lie on her right side in bed, and using the hand gesture described above, practice 10 rounds of Left Nostril Breathing, inhaling and exhaling slowly through the left nostril. I also suggested that she extend the exhale so that it was twice as long as her inhale, which increases the calming effect. I asked her to count backward as she practiced. In our next session, she told me that in the days she had been practicing since our last meeting, she had never yet reached zero before falling asleep. As she continued to practice in bed each night, she was eventually able to discontinue the use of the hand gesture and simply imagine breathing in and out through her left nostril. This is a more subtle but effective variation of Left Nostril Breathing.

BREATH RETENTION (Kumbhaka)

Shirley Telles and her colleagues have studied the effect of breath retention. Their research indicates that short breathing cycles with brief retention energizes the body, while holding the breath longer (up to about 16 counts) calms the body. With short retention, there is "a significant increase (52%) in oxygen consumption and metabolic rate, compared to the pre-pranayamic base-line period of breathing. In contrast, the long kumbhak a [retention] pranayamic breathing caused a statistically significant lowering (19%) of the oxygen consumption and metabolic rate" (Telles & Desiraju, 1991).

When your client is comfortable and steady in her practice of

Yogic Three-Part Breath (Dirga), Ocean-Sounding Victory Breath (Ujjayi), and Alternate-Nostril Purifying Breath (Nadi Shodhana), you may invite her to hold the breath at the top of the inhalation, initially for just a short time, perhaps a count of four. You might also experiment with lengthening the exhalation and pausing briefly before inhaling again. Here is a good beginning ratio that is calming:

1. Inhale for four counts.
2. Hold the breath for four counts.
3. Exhale for six counts.
4. Hold the breath out for two counts.

Modifications

Do not teach a breath retention longer than four counts without laying the groundwork with a few of the calming breath practices described above, like Ocean-Sounding Victory Breath, Yogic Three-Part Breath, and a basic attention to the breath. By the time a longer hold is introduced, your client should already have an understanding, both experiential and intellectual, that managing her breath gives her the power to manage her mood.

Although for most people intentionally holding the breath is calming, some clients may experience panic or a fear of being smothered when the breath is held. In this case, you might suggest holding to two-thirds capacity. If that is still uncomfortable, do not encourage breath retention. When feelings of panic arise during breath retention, it may prove to be fertile ground for inquiry into the client's history about times when she has felt similarly smothered or panicked.

Breath retention can be enhanced by incorporating a soothing visual image (bhavana). Combine a mantra, affirmation, or prayer along with the image, and the effect will likely be increased.

Suggest that your client find a visual image that is soothing and serene, perhaps from nature. If an image doesn't readily come, rather than suggesting an image, invite her to think the word *peace* as she holds her breath. If your client has already stated her intention, invite her to say it to herself like a mantra as she holds the breath. For example, "I am confident and at ease." The retention may be increased after regular practice, but do not guide more than an 8-count hold.

Contraindications

Do not practice breath retention if your client has unmedicated high blood pressure, heart disease, or glaucoma.

Application

Psychotherapist and yoga teacher Joe Walter introduced his client Beth to breath retention gradually, and it proved to be a useful intervention.

Beth is a 34-year-old woman with a long history of depression. She lives with her parents, who actively abused her as a child. She is obese and her health is poor, so she frequently misses work because of her health concerns. When Beth called Joe to schedule an appointment, she told him that she was so tense she could neither relax nor sleep, and she described herself as depressed and overwhelmed.

Joe's first three sessions were dedicated to introducing Beth to simple seated calming breath practices. In the first session, he taught her breath awareness, coaching her to become aware of the breath at the tip of her nostrils as she breathed in and out. Next, he added Ocean-Sounding Victory Breath and Yogic Three-Part Breath as described above. They practiced together in session, and Beth practiced three times a day at home. "When she returned the following week," Joe said, "Beth had experienced significant relief. Her muscles had softened, her tension had subsided, and her mood was beginning to improve." Joe noticed continuing improvement over the next two sessions. In her fourth session, Joe introduced breath retention with a mantra that he and

Beth developed together based on a quote from my book, *Yoga for Depression*, specifically, "Every time I judge myself harshly, I break my own heart."* He taught her to use the mantra in the 4:4:6:2 breath retention pattern described above. "We practiced in session, retaining the breath for four counts while silently experiencing the mantra." At the fifth session, Beth told Joe she had consistently used the 4:4:6:2 breath joined with the mantra at work, where she often engaged in harsh self-judgment. "She reported that the experience of the breath with the mantra was calming and helped her interrupt the negative, harsh self-judgment cycle." In the same session, she told Joe that her new breathing practice and mantra had helped her begin to think more positively about herself. She was paying attention to her diet and in fact was losing weight.

BEE BREATH (Brahmari)

One of the most soothing breathing practices is Bee Breath (*Brahmari*). It cultivates what the yogis call *pratyahara*, a withdrawal of the senses. My students and clients have described it as womblike, blissful, and "like coming home to myself." Bee Breath slows down the exhalation with a constriction of the glottis and a sound. This has a calming effect on the entire nervous system. It can include a mudra or hand gesture that further blocks the outside world and creates a felt sense of going within. Since practicing the breath, especially with the mudra, might seem a bit odd to a client with no familiarity with yoga, you might delay the introduction of Bee Breath until you have established a therapeutic bond and your client has already experienced the difference that breathing practice has made in her life.

---

*The actual quote is: "My beloved child, break your heart no longer. Each time you judge yourself, you break your own heart." Originally attributed to Swami Kripalu, it has since been established that it was written (she uses the word *channeled*) by Vidya Carolyn Dell'uomo, while sitting in meditation with Swami Kripalu sometime between 1970 and 1974.

1. Sit in a comfortable position with the spine erect and the chin pointing slightly downward. Constrict the glottis at the back of your throat by drawing the base of the tongue back. Your lips are closed throughout the practice.
2. Inhale through the nostrils. The emphasis of this practice is on the exhalation. Exhale slowly through the nostrils, making a deep buzzing sound in your throat like a bee.

With the lips closed, your bee will seem to multiply into an entire hive. You will feel the buzzing vibration in your throat. Practice this breath three times to begin and not more than 6 times, as it has such a calming effect that your client may have trouble staying alert enough to drive home.

As your client becomes more comfortable with the breath, you may introduce *Shanmukhi* Mudra (Figure 4.6), a modified Shanmukhi, or simply suggest that your client plug up her ears in whatever way she finds comfortable. Shanmukhi further blocks the senses.

Figure 4.6. Shanmukhi Mudra

Shanmukhi Mudra

1. Frame the face with the inside edges of the hands and place the index fingers directly above the brow, pointing toward the brow point.
2. Rest the middle fingers lightly over the eyelids. (Too much pressure may cause discomfort for those wearing contact lenses.)
3. Place the ring fingers at the edge of the nostrils, without closing the nostrils.
4. Little fingers touch the corners of the closed lips.
5. Plug up the ears by using the thumbs to press the knobby cartilage in front of the ears into the outer ear canals.

Shanmukhi Mudra Modification

Here is the modification, which is simple and easy for your clients to practice in session.

Rub the hands together to warm them, and then place the palms lightly over the eyes to block out ambient light. Suggest that the eyes be closed. Then plug up the ears by using the thumbs to either press the knobby cartilage in front of the ears into the outer ear canals or press the earlobes into the ears. If this is difficult, suggest earplugs. You might keep a supply of foam plugs in your office for this purpose.

Occasionally a client will feel smothered during this practice. You can have her try the practice without the mudra, or simply hum. Again, if feelings of panic arise, it can be fertile ground for inquiry into feelings and history.

Application

Suzanne, Deborah Lubetkin's 40-year-old client suffering from anorexia whom I mentioned in Chapter 1, benefited from breath work in the very first session and was receptive to learning more. As the sessions progressed, it was clear to Dr. Lubetkin that Suzanne came into each session very revved up. Her thoughts were racing, her speech was fast moving, and she had trouble making the transition into the therapy session. "I had carefully assessed her, and she was clearly not bipolar. I had also seen how she was able to calm down significantly after some simple breath work." So Deborah introduced the Bee Breath as a way to help her transition into the session, to decrease the obsessive thought pattern (Figure 4.7). "She

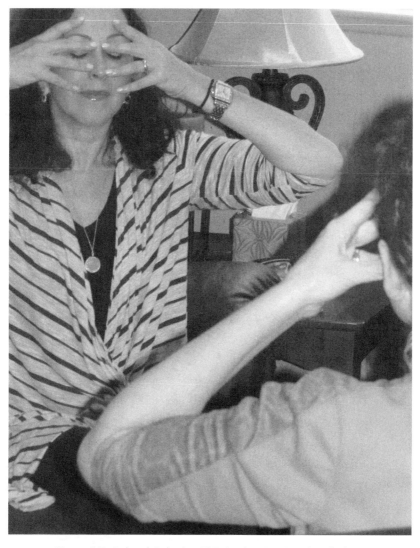

Figure 4.7. Deborah Lubetkin, PhD, leading Bee Breath with client

was very receptive to this, actually becoming silent for the first time since we had met. We continue to use the Bee Breath regularly." After years of vainly attempting to control the world and her own emotions, Suzanne began to feel her emotions instead of simply reacting to them. For the first time, she cried in sessions. "She is always amazed," said Dr. Lubetkin, "by the space she has learned to create in both mind and body."

OTHER CALMING BREATH PRACTICES

Smile Breath

One of the first breathing experiences I teach clients and groups in workshops is the simple Smile Breath. The Vietnamese Buddhist monk Thich Nhat Hanh says, "Sometimes your joy is the source of your smile, or sometimes your smile can be the source of your joy." The body's biochemistry doesn't know the difference between a real smile and a fake one. The same feel-good hormones are given a boost. I discussed this tool in Chapter 1 from the standpoint of establishing a safe container. Because it's so simple and can be used at any time during or between sessions, it's worth repeating here.

1. Inhale, then gradually exhale all the breath through the nose as you lower your chin to your chest.
2. Lift the corners of the month.
3. Inhale and lift the chin.
4. Exhale and open your eyes.

Smile Breath takes less than 10 seconds and it can fundamentally shift your point of view as it soothes the autonomic nervous system. Not only can the Smile Breath be a simple tool to enable your clients to shift their moods, but it can help you refresh and renew your energy as you usher one client out of your office when another is already waiting.

Counting the Breath

A simple technique to calm the busy mind and to center both you and your client is to count breaths together.

1. Notice the breath moving in and out at the tips of the nostrils.
2. Count the beats of your inhalation.
3. Count the beats of your exhalation.
4. Pause to let your client do this.
5. If the body–mind is in a sluggish state, increase the length of the inhalation.
6. If the body–mind is in an overactive state, increase the length of the exhalation.
7. Allow time for several breaths.

As always, when you finish, check in with your client, directing him to notice sensations in the body.

Coherent Breathing

Although not specifically a yoga breathing exercise, one of the simplest and most effective breathing strategies for managing mood is a practice derived from Qigong that is similar to breathing practices taught in yoga. Coherent Breathing was developed by Steve Elliot, a breathing and Qigong teacher in Texas. Research-author-clinician duo Dr. Richard Brown and Dr. Patricia Gerbarg have further developed and integrated Coherent Breathing and other mind–body techniques into their psychiatric practices and into the workshops they offer for health care providers and yoga teachers.

The Coherent Breathing practice is based on pacing the breath so that both inhale and exhale are of an even duration. The ultimate goal of this practice is five to six breaths per minute, or a 6-second inhale and 6-second exhale. This breath encourages balance in the autonomic nervous system (balance of the parasympathetic and sympathetic nervous systems).

1. Inhale for a slow count of four through the nose.
2. Exhale for a slow count of four through the nose.

If you wish to evenly space the breath, in your mind say, "Inhale, 2, 3, 4. Exhale, 2, 3, 4."

CLOSING THE BREATHING PRACTICE

After guiding any of the practices in this book, as your client remains with her eyes closed, ask her to scan her body for sensations and to notice if any thoughts or feelings are arising in her mind. Cue directly to body parts like lips and hands, as this is easier for many for whom attending to the body may be challenging. Before she opens her eyes, ask your client to notice if there's a sharper focus or a more relaxed state. With eyes remaining closed (for most clients), you might cue to these optimum mind-body states for your work together by saying something like, "Notice if the mind is a little clearer, a little calmer. Notice if there's a little more room inside for you." When you invite her to open her eyes, ask her what she notices.

CHAPTER 5

MOOD-ELEVATING BREATH PRACTICES

All of us have times when the energy available just doesn't meet the task. Perhaps you've slept poorly or have a full caseload, clients you're worried about, and a family at home waiting for rides to soccer or gymnastic practice and dinner on the table. You will find that the practices in this chapter may diminish the need for a stop at Starbucks. You may find a favorite to begin your morning, leaving you feeling fresh and awake. Another of these tools may be the perfect pick-me-up between clients. Still another yogic breath may help you clear the slate of what has come before, be it the argument with the third-party payer over an extension of treatment or a client who has been talking of suicide. One minute of breathing practice may be all it takes. And there you are, attuned with your own true nature, compassionate and curious. There you are, once again the unclouded mirror, present and ready to respond in ways that support your next client's journey toward sustaining optimum mental health. Each of the practices included in this chapter is appropriate for your own self-care. Some of the practices will feel right for certain clients and not for others. But don't be surprised when the straitlaced guy in the three–piece suit tells you that the seemingly most esoteric practice in this book is changing his life.

Dan Newman, a psychotherapist in Arizona who specializes in trauma and critical incidents and works primarily with clients in law enforcement, was surprised by just such a circumstance. A high-ranking official in a federal agency, Gary, was referred to him for therapy. Two of Gary's senior agents had committed suicide in the previous year, and his marriage was in trouble due in part to his own infidelity with a coworker. The affair had resulted in a performance review that was threatening to relieve him of his command. He had trouble getting up in the morning to go to work and complained of lethargy and brain fog. Compounding his depression was an untreated trauma reaction. Four years earlier, Gary had been on the scene when a bomb detonated on a bus, killing several people. Since the accident, his use of alcohol had increased. He had trouble sleeping and found himself raging at his wife. Dan's sessions with Gary included eye movement desensitization and reprocessing therapy, and there had been an observable reduction in his trauma-related symptoms, but the underlying depression was more evident than ever. As they concluded their fourth session, Dan led Gary in an easy 4:4 count breath as described in Chapter 4 and then showed him the Power Hara described below. After practicing together for a few minutes, Gary said, "This feels great. Do you have any more of these breathing exercises?" Gary went home with a CD (see Chapter 11). In the next session, he said, "I've been practicing with this CD every day. I have more energy and my mind is clearer." Gary's allotted number of sessions ran out, and Dan hadn't seen him for about 6 months, when he called unexpectedly. "I just want to thank you, Dan," he said. "This yoga breathing has changed my life."

MEETING THE MOOD (AGAIN)

As we discussed in Chapter 3, it's important to meet your client's mood with the yoga tool you offer. Otherwise the client may feel pushed beyond the natural progression toward recognizing her wholeness, her buoyant well-being beneath whatever mood is visiting. The contrast between feeling bad and suddenly feeling good may be so unfamiliar that it's frighting, resulting in a backsliding to a mood state that feels more familiar. If the client overidentifies with the angst, saying things like, "All great writers are depressed," or "I just don't feel like myself. This good mood feels inauthentic," then you've likely moved a little too quickly. The client may even feel manipulated into feeling good. She may tell you that you really don't get her story or how much she is suffering. Or she may feel that you're trying to fix her, which will likely fixate her in her issues. Whatever practices you've introduced will be abandoned until she feels her pain has been fully witnessed and acknowledged.

For this reason, just because many of the following practices are energizing and useful for depression doesn't mean they will always be the best place to start when working with someone who is suffering from depression. Before introducing a more stimulating breath, start with a calming practice as a way of meeting your client where he is. In fact, two breathing practices discussed in Chapter 4 Yogic Three-Part Breath and Ocean-Sounding Victory Breath)are both calming and energizing, so they are an excellent way of introducing your client to the concept of working with the breath to manage the mood.

YOGIC THREE-PART BREATH (Dirga Pranayama) & OCEAN-SOUNDING VICTORY BREATH (Ujjayi)

The instructions for both of these exercises are in Chapter 4. I am including these two breathing practices again here because, although they stimulate the parasympathetic nervous system, slowing down respiration and heart rate, both practices create a state of mental alertness and focus. Before Anne Friedenheim used the more energizing breathing practices with her client Lenore, as discussed in Chapter 2, she first taught her this pattern of deep Yogic Three-Part Breath along with the wave sound characteristic of Ocean-Sounding Victory Breath.

STAIR STEP BREATH (Analoma Krama, Viloma Krama)

Stair Step Breath is a mildly energizing breath that is safe for most people. The activity in the practice gives the busy mind something to do, so it is appropriate for both anxiety and depression.

1. In a sitting or supine position, inhale in little sips or steps of breath from the bottom to the top of the lungs, as though climbing a mountain (usually 6 to 10).
2. Hold for four counts (the top of the mountain).
3. Exhale slowly for six counts.
4. Practice steps 1–3 two times.
5. Next take a smooth six-count breath in.
6. Hold for four counts.
7. Then exhale through the nostrils in little puffs, as though stepping down a mountain (usually 8 to 10).
8. Practice steps 5–7 two times.
9. Next inhale in little sips until the lungs are filled as described above, hold for four counts, and then exhale in little puffs as described above. Practice this version of stepped breathing in and out two times.
10. End by inhaling in little sips, holding for four, and exhaling for six counts or longer. Practice this breathing pattern two times.

This practice is enhanced by incorporating visual imagery (bhavana) and mantra during the retention, which is discussed in Chapters 6 and 8.

Contraindications

Do not practice if your client has had recent abdominal or chest surgery. Practice only on the inhalation if your client is pregnant.

Application

Belinda, a psychotherapist who asked not to be identified beyond her first name, shared a story about her use of Stair Step Breath with an intelligent, academically inclined adolescent boy named Stephen who had been bullied for several years and had no friends. Stephen was not athletic and often felt humiliated in gym class when he was the last to be chosen for a team sport. The bully used the locker room as an opportunity to further shame Stephen for his slight stature and his mannerisms, which the bully identified as gay. Stephen had not experienced attraction to other boys, but the incessant taunts that followed him down the hallway and back into the classroom left him confused about his sexual orientation and deeply embarrassed in his school life.

Belinda worked with Stephen for several months and although his parents had intervened at the school on his behalf and the bully was no longer abusing him, Stephen's depressed mood continued to deepen. He developed one physical symptom after another, and his absences from school increased. He lost interest in his studies and his grades declined. At home he was moody and often provoked fights with his younger sister, who was now accusing him of bullying her.

After Belinda attended LifeForce Yoga training, she incorporated yoga tools into her work with clients and introduced Stephen to Stair Step Breath. She also encouraged his parents to practice it with him and gave them a CD to do so. After 2 weeks of regular practice, Stephen was more energetic and came into sessions talking about guitar lessons. The next week he talked about a new friend who was into the same bands he liked. The friend was on the debating team and encouraged Stephen to join. Within a month, Stephen was working hard at school, had won a debate, and was talking on the phone with a girl on the debating team. By the end of the semester, his grades had improved and Stephen was ready to terminate therapy. He said that he and his friends were signing up for a yoga class the next semester instead of gym.

BREATH OF JOY

Breath of Joy awakens the body, temporarily stimulating the sympathetic nervous system, which acts to mobilize the body's resources with its strong inhalations and arm movements while increasing oxygen levels in the bloodstream. Not only is there an immediate feel-good effect from the release of pent-up tension, but on completion the mind is calm and focused as the parasympathetic system, which sustains the body at rest, kicks in. The result is a state of homeostatic balance between energy and peace.

Breath of Joy can counter the shallow upper-chest breathing of both depression and anxiety, as it automatically invites the breath into all parts of the lungs from the bottom up. Like a strong bright wind, the practice sweeps the dull sluggishness and lethargy of depression from the mind and leaves behind a serene sense of clarity.

1. Stand with feet shoulder width apart and parallel, knees slightly bent, as though about to sit down in a chair.
2. Inhale one-third of your lung capacity through the nostrils as you swing the arms up in front of the body, until they are parallel to each other at shoulder level (Figure 5.1).

Figure 5.1. Breath of Joy 1

Figure 5.2. Breath of Joy 2

3. Continue inhaling to two-thirds capacity and stretch the arms out to the side like wings at shoulder level (Figure 5.2).

4. Inhale to full capacity and swing the arms parallel and over the head, palms facing each other (Figure 5.3).

Figure 5.3. Breath of Joy 3

Figure 5.4. Breath of Joy 4

5. Open the mouth and exhale completely with an audible "ha," bending the knees more deeply as you sink into a standing squat and swing the arms down and back behind you like a diver, palms facing in (Figure 5.4).

Repeat up to nine more times. Don't force or strain the body or breath; simply be absorbed by the peacefully stimulating rhythm. Return to standing, close the eyes, and experience the effects. Notice the heartbeat; feel the sensations in the face and arms, and the tingling in the palms of the hands.

Contraindications
Do not lead this practice if your client has untreated high blood pressure or if there is head or eye injury, migraines, or glaucoma. If the client feels light-headed, instead of lighthearted, advise him to stop for a minute and just breathe normally.

Application
I often suggest this breath for those who have trouble getting out of bed in the morning. "You have to get up to pee," I'll say. "So on the way back to bed, commit to practicing three rounds of Breath of Joy, and see if you have enough energy to keep you from crawling back under the covers."

Felicity Boyer, the LifeForce Yoga Practitioner we met in Chapter 4, helped a client through a difficult time by suggesting she practice this breath while on a family vacation. Before leaving for her trip, Sandy had been verbally abused by someone in an unexpected altercation. She was having difficulty releasing her anger toward this person, and it was interfering with her enjoyment of the vacation. Felicity suggested a vigorous walk on the beach followed by several rounds of Breath of Joy to fling away the toxic energy and shame she had picked up during this exchange. Felicity encouraged Sandy to use a loud, vigorous "ha" as she swept the anger from her body. Following the practice, Felicity recommended several rounds of Left Nostril Breathing to calm her down after the cleansing breath work. When Sandy called the next day, she was happy to report that she hadn't thought of the triggering incident since practicing the breath and that she was finally having a good time with her family.

PULLING PRANA

Pulling Prana is another standing breath practice that like Breath of Joy has a similar effect, raising heart rate and oxygen intake, even as it invokes feelings of clarity and spaciousness upon completion. It's easy to do and needs little instruction.

1. Stand with the feet a comfortable distance apart and, as you inhale through the nostrils, raise the arms over the head with the palms facing each other (Figure 5.5).
2. Exhale and pull the arms down toward your waist,

Figure 5.5. Pulling Prana 1

making fists of the hands. Knees bend softly as you pull (Figure 5.6). Repeat 10–20 times.

3. Extend the arms out in front of the waist with the hands open, on an inhalation (Figure 5.7).

Figure 5.6. Pulling Prana 2

Figure 5.7. Pulling Prana 3

4. Exhale and pull the arms in toward your waist, making fists of the hands. Continue to bend the knees with each pull. Repeat 10–20 times.

5. Alternate arms, as though cross-country skiing, bending the knee opposite the extended arm. Repeat 10–20 times.

Contraindications

Do not lead this practice if your client has untreated high blood pressure.

Application

I recently visited the Holocaust Museum in Washington, DC. The horror of witnessing the exhibit "The Final Solution" on the third floor brought me to tears. The friend with whom I was traveling left the museum in serious back pain, a condition he hadn't experienced in several years. I looked at the frozen faces of the other people exiting the museum and was grateful that, even though I felt awful, I was neither numbing out nor constricting around the horror. Still, along with my friend, I carried a heavy heart out into the Mall.

We had witnessed and acknowledged the inconceivable evil of the Holocaust and the decimation of those 6 million lives, and I told my friend that I felt it was time to release what we had seen and move on with our evening and the plans we had made to go to dinner. We cannot fully be present for those we love and those we serve if we carry the tension of what we witness in the body-mind. Yes, be a witness, whether it's to your client's history of trauma and loss or to scenes from the Holocaust, and then let it go. It's important to have tools to clear the space for yourself as well as for your clients. One of my teachers, yogi and psychologist Richard Miller, says, "If I am clear space, then the barbs of life just don't stick." We may feel the pain along with our clients; we feel our own losses and disappointments. But if we constrict around them, carrying them out of the office or, in this case, into our evening, we not only spoil the time we may have to spend with our loved ones, but we risk making ourselves sick. We need tools to clear the space, so when the barbs of life prick and wound us, we can also remove them.

So right there on the Mall in Washington, DC, I led my friend in Pulling Prana. We added in a few rounds of the Power Hara, described below, and within a few minutes we were laughing at how silly we looked and how much fun we were having. This time the tears rolling down my face were from laughing so hard that my side hurt. My friend's back pain was gone.

BREATH TO STIMULATE THE NERVES

This is a simple breathing practice that is easy to instruct and gives a felt sense of energy in the body. It may be especially valuable for clients for whom it has not felt safe to live in the body since their abuse.

1. Inhale to two-thirds capacity as you extend arms out from the waist and make fists.
2. Without breathing, pump the arms toward the torso.

After you've led the client through this practice in the safe and supportive environment of your consultation room, you can cue her to feel the sensations in her arms, her hands, and her face, without ever using the word *safe*. In those moments when she is feeling that sensation, she has leaped across the misbelief that it's not safe to feel.

Contraindications
Do not lead this practice if your client has untreated high blood pressure.

Application
Several years ago, I was working with a yoga therapy client who had recently terminated psychotherapy. Working in psychotherapy,

Jeanne had uncovered an early sexual abuse memory involving her beloved grandfather. The pain of that recovered memory had thrown her into a flurry of emotional eating. When she realized how much weight she was gaining, she abruptly quit therapy. She had also just entered a rigorous doctoral program in neuroscience that demanded so much mental energy that it made it easy not to feel. She wanted a yoga program to support her focus and to help her lose weight and had committed to three yoga therapy sessions to do so. She did not come to yoga sessions wanting to feel more.

I told her that we would together develop a practice for her that was energizing and would likely help her meet her goals. I also explained that when we pay attention to body sensation and breath, sometimes emotions arise—tears are not uncommon on the yoga mat. But generally, the tears are not connected to the story. They are releasing and refreshing, and most people feel better afterward. She was wary at first, afraid that if tears erupted, she wouldn't be able to stop them. This is a common feeling among clients—if they let themselves feel, the pain will be so overwhelming that they will be carried out of the room in a straitjacket.

In our first session, I showed Jeanne some standing pranayama breathing to clear her mind and heighten her focus for her work. I also knew that these energizing breathing practices were likely to dissolve some of her unconscious as well as conscious prohibitions against feeling.

In our second session, after practicing Breath to Stimulate the Nerves, Jeanne stood, feeling the sensations in her arms, her palms, and her fingertips. I had her breathe the sensation down into her feet, grounding her. As she did so, she began to cry softly. She opened her eyes and said, "I just realized that I haven't felt my body for a long time. I've been living from the neck up."

"How does it feel?" I asked.

"Good," she whispered. At her next session, Jeanne said that she had been practicing all week, sometimes feeling so grateful to be living in her body again that she cried. She also told me that she had called her psychotherapist for an appointment. The yoga practice had allowed her to sense her body and begin to access her emotions in a safe enough way that she wasn't flooded by them and could resume the work of therapy.

POWER HARA

The standing energizing breath of Power Hara adds a twist, which can feel very good for a stiff spine. It brings more oxygen into the lungs with two concurrent deep breaths and stimulates the midsection of the body. Often in depression the shoulders are slumped, the spine may round, and there's a sluggishness at the solar plexus. In yoga, we think of the solar plexus (manipura chakra) as the seat of self-esteem, identity, and power. The Power Hara cranks up the battery at the solar plexus, increasing a sense of vitality and personal power.

1. Stand with your feet slightly wider than hip width apart and bring your hands to your shoulders with your elbows pointed out like chicken wings.
2. Inhale, filling your lungs halfway, and twist to the left (Figure 5.8). Inhale fully and twist to the right.
3. Extend your right arm forcefully to the left as you twist to the left, exhaling through your mouth with a vigorous "ha" sound (Figure 5.9).
4. Extend your left arm forcefully to the right as you twist to the right, exhaling again through your mouth with a "ha" sound.

Figure 5.8. Power Hara 1

Figure 5.9. Power Hara 2

5. Practice 10 full rounds. Release, close your eyes, and feel your awakened energy.

Contraindications

Do not practice this exercise with anyone who has had recent abdominal surgery or is pregnant.

Application

As I mentioned in Chapter 1, I used to volunteer at the Juvenile Detention Center in Tucson, teaching a weekly yoga class to girls ages 12 to 18. Between their heavy, carb-laden diets and the medications most of them were given, the girls shuffled in like elderly patients on a psych ward. To combat their sluggish feelings, I incorporated many mood-elevating breath practices with them.

I met their mood with a slow start, sitting on mats in a circle and sharing names and one small thing they were grateful for, or one or two words to describe how they were feeling. Words like *tired* and *sad* were the norm. We built the energy slowly to a standing position. Once we were standing, I knew we could shift the energy, clearing out the heaviness and lethargy in the room with a few rounds of Pulling Prana or Power Hara. The girls loved the Power Hara. For a few moments, it gave them a sense of control over their feelings of powerlessness. After practicing several rounds, they were brighter and more engaged, with a calm focus we developed through the rest of the class.

BELLOWS BREATH (Bhastrika)

Bellows Breath is practiced in a seated position and is especially good for depression. The subjective experience is one of mild elation, followed by a feeling of relaxation. During practice, the sympathetic nervous system is briefly stimulated. However, following practice, the parasympathetic system is awakened. Blood pressure and heart rate usually drop below the resting rate.

Various yoga traditions teach Bellows Breath differently. But in all traditions, both inhalation and exhalation are deep and forceful. The breath is most safely instructed at the rate of one inhalation and one exhalation per second. Increasing the speed risks producing an overstimulating effect that can actually raise anxiety levels and trigger a manic response among bipolar I clients with a propensity toward mania.

1. Sit comfortably with your spine erect. Bend your elbows and make fists with your hands, bringing them to your shoulders so that the knuckles face out, with the forearms and upper arms hugging the torso. Take a normal natural breath in and out.
2. As you inhale through the nostrils, send your arms straight up, over your head with great force, opening your palms to face outward and spreading your fingers wide (Figure 5.10).

Figure 5.11. Bellows Breath 2

Figure 5.10. Bellows Breath 1

3. Exhale with great force through the nostrils as you bring your arms back to the starting position again, making fists with your hands (Figure 5.11).
4. Do this at a moderate pace 20 times, and then rest for 30 seconds. You may practice two more rounds of 20 each, pausing for at least 30 seconds between rounds.
5. When you have completed the practice, sit for several moments, observing the effects.

Modifications & Contraindications

Do not practice Bellows Breath if you or your client has unmedicated high blood pressure. If there is shoulder soreness or injury, practice Bellows Breath with the arms coming forward and back in front of the chest.

Application

Sharon was suffering from an anxiety-based depression when she came to me for yoga therapy, referred by her psychiatrist. Not only was Sharon an accomplished technical writer with many publication credits in engineering journals, but she had recently retired as a director at a global engineering firm. When I met her, she did not maintain eye contact. Her speech was slow, and she was extremely self-judging. This intelligent, creative woman spoke of her stupidity for moving to a new community after her divorce from a critical man not unlike her father. Thinking that the sunlight would encourage her to be outdoors and would lift her mood, she had moved to Tucson from the Northeast, far from her two sons and their families, and she was feeling isolated and alone. We used a number of yoga tools to help her deal with insomnia and her mood disorder. I encouraged her to join a yoga class at the Jewish Community Center as a way of meeting like-minded, like-hearted people with whom she might have more in common than the class she had tried at a fitness-oriented gym populated by younger people.

Bellows Breath was especially helpful to her in the morning when she had trouble motivating herself to get out of the house. When we practiced it in sessions, there was an immediate change in her appearance. Her spine was straighter, her eyes were bright, and she was making eye contact. After practicing Bellows Breath at home, she had more energy and began riding a bike to the JCC, where she eventually made friends in yoga class and at other social events.

Bellows Breath has been effective in working with clients with a history of trauma. Patricia Rogers, a clinical social worker in Norwood, Massachusetts, had been working with a client with a history of sexual abuse for several years when she introduced Bellows Breath. After the second round of Bellows Breath, Patricia asked her to notice how she was feeling. "He can't stop me from breathing," her client said. "I can breathe the way I want to!"

Patricia said that her client's spontaneous verbalization was "quite astonishing for both of us. She felt empowered in a way she had never felt before."

UNILATERAL RIGHT NOSTRIL BREATHING
(Surya Bheda)

Just as Left Nostril Breathing, described in Chapter 4, calms the autonomic nervous system, Right Nostril Breathing is more stimulating (Raghuraj & Telles, 2008; Telles et al., 1994). I often practice Right Nostril Breathing when feeling groggy on a long drive or, if I feel tired, before giving a talk. This breathing practice is easy to teach to your clients and is especially recommended for depression.

The safest, easiest way to practice this form of unilateral breathing is to breathe 4 counts in through the right nostril and 4 counts out through the left, regulating the airflow between nostrils with the right-hand fingers in the hand gesture described in Chapter 4 (Vishnu Mudra; Figure 4.3).

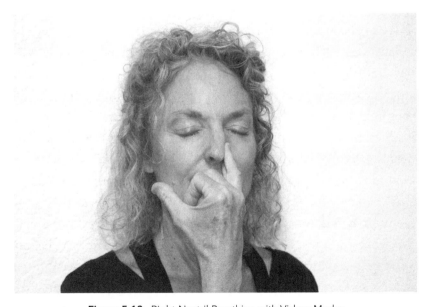

Figure 5.12. Right Nostril Breathing with Vishnu Mudra

1. Begin with the fourth and fifth fingers of the right hand closing the left nostril as you inhale through the right nostril.
2. Cover the right nostril with the thumb of the right hand and exhale through the left nostril.
3. Repeat this pattern up to 20 times.

There are variations of unilateral breathing that keep the breath moving through the right nostril for both inhalation and exhalation. The effect is stronger, so if practicing Right Nostril Breathing in this way, be sure to conclude with a few rounds of Alternate-Nostril Purifying Breath.

Modifications

If the right nostril is occluded, apply pressure with the right thumb at the base and to the side of the nostril while practicing.

Application

Mark, a lawyer and yoga teacher who described himself as a "type A personality," had recently gone through a divorce and came to me to learn additional yoga tools to help him with the depression he was feeling. He taught Bikram Yoga, a tightly scripted and vigorous style of yoga practiced in a heated room that includes a sequence of 24 postures, each done twice. It's a style that often appeals to athletes and those wanting to get in shape. Although a class can have a deeply meditative effect, the class itself is low on meditation and soothing messages. After sweating through a Bikram class, where instructions are delivered in a crisp drill-sergeant manner, practitioners usually feel lighter and more energized. I know this firsthand as in my 40s, I was both a practitioner and a teacher of the style.

Mark loved his Bikram practice but wanted to learn some simple ways to feel better when he didn't have time to roll out a mat. We worked with several of the breathing practices in this chapter, a few of the calming practices outlined in the last chapter, and the mudras and mantras in the chapters that follow. The easiest practice for him to use in his office, between clients and whenever he felt his mood and his energy slump, was Right Nostril Breathing, which he did vigorously, as he did most things in his life. I encouraged him to practice alternate-nostril nadhi sodhana after this unilateral breathing practice, so that he would feel more balanced.

Contraindications

There are, of course, many breathing practices that are not appropriate for a clinical setting. I'll review a few of them here, without instructions. These practices are very energizing and have a number of contraindications. They should not be taught or practiced without proper instruction by a knowledgeable yoga teacher or yoga therapist who is experienced and trained in the instruction of pranayama breathing and its effects.

These practices include vigorous belly-pumping breaths like Skull Polishing (*Kapalabhati*), Belly Rolling (*Uddiyana Bandha* and *Agni Sara*) Belly Churning (*Nauli*), the Kundalini Breath of Fire, and the Art of Living Sudarshan Kriya practice. While all of these are good for depression, practicing in excess or without proper supervision can throw someone with a predisposition for mania into a manic state. These practices are therefore not recommended for those suffering from bipolar I or high levels of anxiety.

CHAPTER 6

THE YOGA OF SOUND (Mantra)

A mantra is a repeated word or sound that gives the mind a calm focus and helps the body relax. Mantras have been used in yoga for thousands of years. Some mantras have religious significance, as in a prayer to a deity, and some do not. The mantras suggested here are universal sounds and tones without religious meaning.

WHY WORK WITH MANTRAS?

There are many reasons to consider introducing sound in a session, not the least of which is that when someone has difficulty breathing deeply, using sound can support an optimum respiratory rate. Using a tone facilitates drawing in a deeper breath and letting it out slowly, both of which calm the body-mind. In my earlier book, *Yoga for Depression* (Weintraub, 2004), I introduced Penny Smith, who successfully interrupted her daughter's panic attack by inviting her to sing "Ee-I-ee-I-oh." When someone is hyperventilating, it is impossible to stop and take a deep breath. But to sing a tone or a musical phrase, we naturally draw in a deeper than normal breath, leaping over the body-mind's inhibition. And when we sing a tone, be it a phrase from "Old MacDonald" or a Sanskrit mantra, we let the breath out slowly, another way of calming the agitation. I once stood in the produce aisle of Trader Joe's singing "yam" with an anxious student who was on the verge of a panic attack. It worked.

According to Luciano Bernardi, professor of internal medicine at the University of Pavia, "The benefits of respiratory exercises to slow respiration in the practice of yoga have long been reported, and mantras may have evolved as a simple device to slow respiration, improve concentration, and induce calm" (Bernardi et al., 2001). In his pivotal study on sound, Bernardi demonstrated that both the "Ave Maria" prayer in Latin and the Sanskrit prayer "*Om mani padme om*" synchronize inherent cardiovascular rhythms and slow respiration to almost six breaths per minute, which is the ideal rate for parasympathetic activation and therefore, as the authors noted, induces favorable psychological and possibly physiological effects, including increasing the arterial baroreflex, which is a favorable prognostic factor in long-term studies in cardiac patients. Bernardi's findings that the beneficial effects of the rosary are identical to those of Sanskrit mantra chanting are not surprising in that the rosary prayer, prayed on beads that resemble the Indian *mala*, was "introduced to Europe by the crusaders, who took it from the Arabs, who in turn took it from Tibetan monks and the yoga masters of India" (Bernardi et al., 2001).

It is interesting that when chanted in Italian, the rosary prayer did not have the same benefits as the same prayer in Latin and the chant in Sanskrit. Could it be that in addition to the optimum breathing pattern of six respirations per minute created by the chant, the universal sounds of ancient languages like Sanskrit, which is the root of all Indo-European languages, and other early faith-imbued languages like Latin, Aramaic, and Hebrew, have a more soothing effect than vernacular languages? We might be convinced of this possibility by looking at the case of deteriorating health conditions among the monks at a Benedictine monastery in the south of France in the 1960s. The monks began to exhibit signs of depression and fatigue. Many fell ill and some died of a variety of diseases. It was clear that something was affecting their immune systems. Their diets, their sleep patterns, and other environmental factors were changed, but nothing ameliorated their condition until Alfred Tomatis, internationally known otolaryngologist and inventor, asked the simple question: What changed in terms of sound? In 1962 Vatican II changed the chanting of the Mass from Latin to the vernacular. When the monks, who had a lifetime of daily chanting of those resonant Latin sounds, began chanting in French, their immune systems were adversely impacted. When Latin chant was reintroduced at the monastery, the health problems abated (Le Mée, 1994).

According to Mitchell Gaynor, director of medical oncology and integrative medicine at Strang-Cornell Cancer Prevention Center and the author of *Sounds of Healing*, sound affects healing in several ways. "It alters cellular functions and biological systems, through entrainment, to function more homeostatically; it calms the mind and the body; [and] affects the emotions, which influence neurotransmitters and neuropeptides, which in turn regulate the immune system" (Gaynor, 2000, p. 47).

You may have seen Masaru Emoto's holographic photographs of water crystals in beautiful mandala-like patterns in response to words like "Om" or "love." After exposing water samples to various sounds including classical and heavy metal music, and mantra tones and prayers, Emoto froze the samples and compared the resulting water crystals. Soothing words and sounds created balanced crystals in the frozen water samples, but harsh sounds and angry words did not. Our bodies are 70 – 80% fluid. If you think of your body as a giant petri dish, you might imagine the impact of soothing sound on that 70–80%. As Dr. Emoto's photographs demonstrate in water, we can theorize that the soothing sounds do calm us, or at least the 70-80% that is fluid, and active consonant-based sounds are likely more stimulating (Emoto & Thayne, 2004).

UNDERSTANDING THE BASICS OF SANSKRIT LETTERS & SOUNDS

The very nature of the Sanskrit language seems to be based on a profound understanding of sound. Sanskrit, composed of 52 letters, is a psychological as well as a physical language. Each letter is the root of a verb and therefore contains within it the energy of all doing and being. The very sounds of Sanskrit mirror their meanings, as do the words themselves. Take for example the word *shanti*, which means peace. In every culture, the "shhh" sound is used to ask for quiet. Quieting voices, both outer and inner, brings peace. In Sanskrit, the consonants represent the external world and are therefore more energizing. You will feel this for yourself when you try out the sounds recommended below. The vowels represent the internal world and are therefore more calming and cooling. In a yoga posture, sound has the ability to take us deeper into a pose, connecting us to what we are feeling and where we are feeling it, and to release chronic tension at deeper levels. You can use these tones in your office to either charge the central nervous system or to soothe and calm it. The mantras from Sanskrit that I am recommending for clinical practice are universal sounds, not prayers, so they can be adapted to any belief system. These simple tones are known as *bija* mantras, which means "seed."

HOW TO INTRODUCE SOUND TO YOUR CLIENT

When introducing anything new, it's good to have the evidence for efficacy at hand. You might have a handout that cites Dr. Bernardi's research or a book recommendation like *The Sounds of Healing* (Gaynor, 2000) or *The Mozart Effect* by Don Campbell (1997). If your client is already interested in yoga, Russill Paul's (2004) *The Yoga of Sound* or *Mantra Yoga and Primal Sound* by David Frawley (2010) are good suggestions. Seeing the evidence and learning more about the effects of sound can bolster your client's willingness to try a new approach. Or, as many of the therapists I've trained have done, you can simply throw out an invitation: "Would you like to try a different approach to calming yourself down when you are feeling uptight and anxious? Let me know if it is uncomfortable in any way. We're going to use a few universal tones that have been shown to soothe the autonomic nervous system." In other words, you don't have to say, "Let's chant Sanskrit!"

For someone unfamiliar with yoga or mantra, you might begin with the universal tone "ah," common to *amen* and also to *namaha*, which means "praise to" in Sanskrit. Invite your client to place a hand on her belly and sing the low tone "ah" along with you. The calming effect will be immediate. You might then invite her to add an "mmm" sound at the end of "ah." The "mmm" sound is soothing. In many cultures, it is an important part of the word for mother—mama, emma, amma, ma. Nothing foreign or strange has been suggested, and you are already making sounds with your client. As it is the last letter of the Sanskrit alphabet, and A is the first, there's a sense of fullness, a feeling of completion when practicing this sound.

PSYCHOLOGICAL ASPECTS OF THE ENERGY CENTERS: NADIS & CHAKRAS

Long before X-rays and CAT scans, yogis understood that there were centers in the human body where the endocrine system and the nerve plexus (the network of intersecting nerves) met. These are called chakras, and they are places where energy is magnified. My book *Yoga for Depression* (Weintraub, 2004) has a more thorough discussion of the chakra system and the nadis. Yogis also understood that our traumas, losses, environmental factors, and everyday challenges can create disturbances at these centers that contribute to imbalances and disease. The ancients designed a system of sounds, movements, and meditations to help clear those disturbances, some of which I've included here and in the next chapter. Before we launch into the tones for calming and stimulating, it will help to have a basic understanding of the psychological aspect of the chakra system itself.

There are hundreds of chakras, but the seven main energy centers, listed below, are the most commonly understood. In Western science they relate to the endocrine glands to a certain extent and also to the nerve plexus. They are not strictly physical, energy based, or metaphysical. The chakras exist equally in the realm of mind, body, and spirit.

1. The root chakra, *muladhara,* is at the base of the spine. It is associated with the color red and, from a psychological point of view, it correlates to secure attachment. When the root chakra is in balance, we feel comfortable in our primary relationships and safe. When the root chakra is in balance we feel secure that our basic survival needs—food, shelter, water—will be met. There is an inner feeling that the "good-enough" mother is at home. The root chakra in balance enables us to connect authentically with others. We think of the heart chakra as being the chakra of compassion and love. But if there is disruption in the root chakra because of trauma in childhood, for example, there could be a lifelong inability to feel nourished in relationships. Early childhood trauma can disrupt that sense of deep connection. Muladhara relates to the earth, and if we are out of sync, if muladhara is not in balance, we may feel ungrounded. When our root chakra is out of balance, we may feel a sense of separation, another reason, from the yogic point of view, that we become depressed. When the root chakra is in gear, we are feeling connected to who we really are, which is so much more than the current mood. A balanced root chakra enables us to feel at home in the world—rooted, grounded, and connected to others.

2. The second chakra is *swadhisthana* at the pelvic region, which is associated with the color orange. When it's in balance we feel comfortable with our sensual self, and with our gender identity and our sexuality. Again, trauma may disrupt that sense of ease. If the chakra is not balanced, there can be sexual addiction at one extreme or sexual withdrawal on the other. There may be fear and guilt around sex. If we have been traumatized,

or simply frightened, we often constrict this area of the body. The psoas muscle, which is one of the largest muscles of the body and connects the upper body to the lower body and the back of the body to the front, tightens. This can constrict the diaphragm and affect our ability to breathe comfortably. If the psoas is tight it may also affect our ability to relax and enjoy our sexuality. The psoas is positioned in the area of the second and third chakra.

3. The third chakra, *manipura*, is located at the solar plexus. The color associated with this chakra is golden yellow, like the sun. When the third chakra is in balance we have a basic sense of healthy self-esteem. We have a sense of our identity in the world. When manipura is not in balance, we can feel depleted. Our adrenals may literally be depleted. If this chakra is under-stimulated, we can feel really stuck in our lives, shut down, and depressed. If there is too much energy, we may seem pretty egotistical to others.

4. The fourth chakra, in the region of the heart, is *anahata*, associated with the color green. When this chakra is in balance, we feel compassion; we are able to forgive, and there's a sense of optimisim. When anahata is out of balance we may cling to old wounds and the sense of being a victim, or we may be stuck in a relationship that is no longer serving us. There can be vengefulness. When it is functioning well, there is self-acceptance, compassion, forgiveness, understanding, and trust.

5. The fifth chakra, *vishuddha*, is at the throat but includes the ears, and is associated with the color blue. In balance, it is about truthfulness, self-expression, and compassionate listening. When I am teaching, I like to do a little soothing of vishuddha chakra, not only because I am speaking and my throat might get sore, but I want to be open and available to listen with compassion, to really hear when I am with a group. When vishuddha chakra is in balance we can listen deeply, communicate our feelings, and fully express our connection with others.

6. The sixth chakra is *ajna* at the brow point, which is associated with the color violet. In balance, ajna chakra is about intuition, intelligence, and confidence. It is where psychological disturbances manifest most clearly. Anxiety, depression, and dementia all show up here. When ajna chakra is in balance, we are intuitive and we trust that inner wisdom.

7. The seventh chakra is *sahasrara* at the crown of the head and is associated with the color white. This is our most spiritual chakra. When we are in balance, we feel our connection to the divine, to the cosmos, or however you define that which is bigger than we are. Physicists tell us that we are compressed energy and that the energy that surrounds us is not any different than the energy flowing through us. When sahasrara is activated, we are aware of that. We are aware of how much bigger we are than the limits of our physical bodies.

Energy or *prana* is carried from the lower chakras to the upper chakras through the nadis or energy channels. These are nonphysical energy conduits sometimes related to the acupuncture meridians. Although there are something like 72,000 nadis, three main ones are worth mentioning: (1) the *ida*, which means comfort, runs on the left side of the body; (2) the *pingala*, which means tawny, runs on the right side of the body; and (3) the *sushumna* nadi, which runs through the center of the body, connecting the root chakra to the crown. The ida and pingala nadis spiral around the sushumna nadi at each of the chakras, and the three major nadis meet at the brow point (ajna chakra).

The ida nadi correlates with the left nostril and runs down the left side of the spine. This is considered to be the yin side, controlled by the right lunar, creative, nonverbal side of the brain. As discussed in Chapter 5, the parasympathetic nervous system can be stimulated with left nostril breathing.

The pingala nadi correlates to the right nostril and runs down the right side of the spine. It is controlled by the left hemisphere of the brain, which is associated with yang energy. The left brain is more orderly, linear, and verbal, and is sometimes associated with masculine energy. These energies meet and can be brought back into balance at the chakras and are carried up the spine through the central channel, the sushumna nadi.

Science is beginning to corroborate what the yogis understood about the chakras thousands of years ago. In researching his book, *Meditation as Medicine,* (Khalsa, 2001), Dharma Singh Khalsa came across Dr. Valerie Hunt's research at UCLA, which used EMG electrodes connected to telemetry equipment to detect energy in the chakras. She found that high-frequency oscillations were coming from the chakras: 1,600 oscillations per second as compared to 200 per second from other parts of the body (Khalsa, 2001).

Although there is no scientific evidence yet, and it may be next to impossible to measure directly, it has long been understood in yoga that, depending on the sound chosen, the vibratory quality of a tone can either stimulate or calm the chakras. The best anecdotal evidence I know comes from my cat, Smokey. When working with Rosie, a long-term client who adored my kitty, I often allowed Smokey to wander through the room where we were practicing. One day, while I was leading Rosie through a relaxation on her back, I decided to use the calming chakra tones as a portal to deep relaxation. Smokey had never climbed on Rosie's belly before, but she did this time, and since I saw a gentle smile play at the corners of Rosie's mouth, I let Smokey stay where she was. Smokey settled in low on Rosie's pelvis, and when Rosie and I began to tone up the chakra system, Smokey moved up too. When we reached the throat chakra, Smokey climbed off, curling up beside Rosie's head for the rest of the relaxation.

COOLING SOUND, CALM MIND

Although there are many cooling mantras and tones in Sanskrit, we will confine ourselves to universal tones common to most languages that are without reference to deities. Although yogis maintain that every practice, including these tones, ultimately connects the practitioner to the deeper rhythms and essential harmony of the universe, the sounds in this chapter do not have a direct religious significance and can be comfortably used by those of all faiths, including devout Christians, Orthodox Jews, Muslims, and Hindus. The cooling, calming tones for the chakras are shown in Table 6.1.

TABLE 6.1. Calming Tones for the Chakras

CHAKRA	MANTRA	ISSUE
Chakra 1 Muladhara (Base of spine)	Ō as in go	Attachment
Chakra 2 Svadhisthana (Lower abdomen)	Ū as in you	Sexuality
Chakra 3 Manipura (Solar plexus)	Ah as in paw	Self-esteem/identity
Chakra 4 Anahata (Heart)	Ā as in pay	Love/self-acceptance
Chakra 5 Vishuddha (Throat)	Ē as in tea	Communication
Chakra 6 Ajna (Third eye)	Mmm	Mood
Chakra 7 Sahasrara (Crown of head)	Hnng	Spirituality

Application

There are numerous ways to use the calming tones both separately and together. For example, if your client's thinking is agitated and he is jumping from thought to thought, you might suggest that he bring his attention to his brow point and begin a humming sound as a way of self-soothing. If he is expressing emotional pain, you might suggest that he bring his hand to his heart and make the long low tone "A." If your client is feeling lonely and isolated, you might suggest the low tone "Ō."

I had several sessions with a New Yorker in her late 30s who had a volatile position in finance. Katie had been in therapy for 11 years and had been taking an antidepressant since the birth of her daughter 6 years earlier. Her anxiety was so high that she had not been able to have intercourse with her husband since her daughter's birth. She loved her husband and wanted to be a full partner with him in their sexual intimacy. Katie made good use of the cooling tones. She practiced them in poses on the mat, when tense at work, and as a way to relax in bed with her husband. Together, they experimented with the tones in their foreplay and after a week of practice, Katie felt sufficiently at ease that their intercourse resumed.

HEATING SOUND, ENERGIZED MIND

While the calming tones are useful, the energizing tones may be more versatile, in that you can change their effect by the way you use them. These tones are commonly thought of in the Western understanding of yoga as the bija mantras, however bija means "seed," and so the word can actually refer to any of the simple mantra tones. Repeating a tone, for example, "lum, lum, lum, lum, lum" for the root chakra, will be more stimulating than extending one long "lum," with emphasis on the seed sound in the letter L (llllllllum). Chanting one long sound is not only more meditative, it is also more grounding. The stimulating tones are shown in Table 6.2. Note that the chakra tones are most often written as "lam, vam,

TABLE 6.2. Stimulating Tones for the Chakras

CHAKRA	MANTRA	ISSUE
Chakra 1 Muladhara (Base of spine)	Lum (red)	Attachment
Chakra 2 Svadhisthana (Lower abdomen)	Vum (orange)	Sexuality
Chakra 3 Manipura (Solar plexus)	Rum (yellow)	Self-esteem/identity
Chakra 4 Anahata (Heart)	Yum (green)	Love/self-acceptance
Chakra 5 Vishuddha (Throat)	Hum (blue)	Communication
Chakra 6 Ajna (Third eye)	Om (violet)	Mood
Chakra 7 Sahasrara (Crown of head)	Nnng (white)	Spirituality

ram, yam, ham, om" and sometimes "ng"; however, they are more resonant and meditative when pronounced as shown in Table 6.2.

Application

You might use the mantra "lum" in a long, nonrepetitive way when working with a client who feels scattered and ungrounded, or who expresses the belief, "I don't belong here." On the other hand, you might use the mantra "vum" in a repetitive way with someone who has a slowed-down libido, as is common in depression and also in those on some antidepressants in the SSRI category. If the mantra is repeated, it can be more activating. If the seed sound "v" is repeated by itself, as in "vë, vë, vë, vë, vë, vë," the second chakra at the pelvic region is stimulated even more than if you repeat the entire mantra. The "m" at the end of the tone softens it, so the most stimulating effect is achieved by repeating the consonant only. As you try it yourself, you will feel a physical response in this area of the body.

Clinical psychologist and yoga teacher Barbara Rowe was working with a teenager named Carla and her family in a treatment center in northern Virginia. In the family sessions Carla refused to talk, and in their individual sessions Carla sat in a slumped position, her voice barely a whisper. Barbara felt they weren't progressing in therapy, so she asked Carla if she would like to try something different. Carla agreed to stand and Barbara guided her into a Warrior II pose (*Virabhadrasana*; Figure 6.1). At first she continued to slump and rolled her eyes when Barbara suggested she use "ram," the energizing tone for the solar plexus. With encouragement and with Barbara practicing alongside her, Carla's voice grew louder as she repeated the tone. Her posture straightened and her eyes came into sharper focus as her extended arms straightened.

Afterward, she smiled but did little talking. Barbara felt discouraged at first, but when she called Carla's mother and sister into the room, the change in Carla was startling. Without prompting, she began speaking about her angry feelings toward her father for being so abusive toward her mother, and her wish that her mother would take a stronger stand in the household. The session became a lively exchange, and therapy progressed over the next few months in a way that was useful to Carla and her family.

You can stay with the secular tones or, if you and your client are open to bringing more spirituality into your sessions, the following tones can be used to enhance the depth of your connection to each other and to an energy beyond the limits of your individual

Figure 6.1. Warrior II Pose

body-minds. To explain this connection, I like Einstein's famous quote written in a 1950 letter to a distraught father who had lost his young son, "A human being is a part of the whole, called by us, 'Universe,' a part limited in time and space. He experiences himself, his thoughts and feelings as something separated from the rest—a kind of optical delusion of his consciousness. This delusion is a kind of prison for us . . ." (Calaprice, 2005, p. 206) Or as the well-known author and psychiatrist Dan Siegel paraphrases, "We are living under the optical delusion of our separateness, and it's lethal" (Siegel, speaking at the Psychotherapy Networker Symposium, 2009). Repeating this to your client might be a way to provide Western validation to this important, foundational yoga concept.

OM

Om is the primordial healing mantra, a sound that some believe to have been the sound of creation, emitted at the moment of the big bang. It is a sound that connects individual consciousness to the consciousness of the cosmos, the Absolute.

Application

This mantra is calming and focusing. If your client is a yoga practitioner or is interested in yoga, beginning or ending a session with Om may add an appreciated spiritual dimension to your work together.

SO HAM

The mantra so ham signifies that there is no separation between the energy that surrounds you and the energy that you are. It means, "I am that."

Application

This mantra and its meaning enhance the effect of working with visual imagery (see Chapter 8).

MAHAHA

The tone mahaha is taken from the mantras that traditionally prepare the mind, body, and spirit to chant the ancient Gayatri mantra. It is a sound that stimulates the energy of the heart chakra, and it encourages laughter.

Application

You might try this mantra in Seated Mountain pose. You will feel the vibration in the solar plexus (manipura chakra) and the cardiac plexus (anahata chakra), and it may even make your client laugh. It has an empowering effect.

NAMAHA

Nam means name in Sanskrit. In this mantra, we are bowing to all that is highest within, not separate from the divine.

Application

If your client is a yoga practitioner or is interested in the spiritual aspects of yoga, this mantra may serve to remind him of his own true nature—the ultimate healer within. With the arms overhead, try drawing the palms through the center line of the body to the heart while slowly chanting this mantra.

USING SOUND WITH CHILDREN

Children respond well to the effect of sound and are usually agreeable to making it. Using tones with a child or a group of children can harness and calm their energy. When I taught youth in juvenile detention in Tucson, the teens loved to make the mantra sounds, and doing so created an oasis of calm for the class to proceed. Laurie Schaeffer, a holistic nurse in Alaska who integrates yoga therapy in her work with children affected by autism, uses tones to great effect. Five years ago, I mentored Laurie, and I wept to see the videotape of her session with a severely autistic 7-year-old boy, who entered the treatment room with arms flailing and making noise. By the end of the session, they were sitting knee to knee, rocking toward each other, using the mantra om. There were even moments of eye contact between the young boy and Laurie. Today, he is 12 years old and continues to meet with Laurie monthly. "You would be amazed," Laurie told me recently. "He is a brilliant ray of light, growing into a wonderful young man."

Joy Bennett, the yoga therapist in Providence, Rhode Island, whom we met in Chapter 1, uses the cooling tones to good effect in her yoga classes that serve children who carry labels like attention deficit disorder, learning disabilities, depression, bipolar disorder, and autism. When she arrives for her class at the special needs school, the chaos of 11 boys in the room can be unsettling. She meets the high energy with movement and sound and then guides her rambunctious young students into a forward bend (calming for the central nervous system) with the cooling, calming tones. "The children enjoy using sound in class," Joy says, "because most of the day, they are told to be quiet." She makes the movement with sound fun and engaging. She might say, "Let's add some soothing sounds to our forward bend today . . . some sounds that can swim around all those watery places inside you. . . . Let's try the sounds of 'Oh-oo-ah' as we bend forward this time." They respond to Joy's instruction well, so she decides to add a couple more sounds, saying, "That was great, everybody! Let's see if we can add even more sounds that can help you feel calm. We'll fold forward with 'oh-oo-ah-ay-ee.'"

One added benefit when you use sound with children is that you can exercise your own vocal cords without the fear of being told, as so many were in their mandatory chorus experience in elementary school, to simply "mouth the words." You don't have to sing a mantra in tune.

I have found that the best mantras to use with children are the simple chakra tones in this chapter—either the grounding tones or the calming, cooling tones, depending on the outcome you wish to achieve.

CHAPTER 7

MUDRAS FOR MANAGING MOOD

Did you know that the human hand contains 2,500 nerve receptors per square centimeter? The tips of our fingers contain more nerve endings than most other parts of the body. The yogis understood that hand gestures called mudras guide energy flow and send messages to the brain. After centuries of study, they understood that each finger, the pressure applied, and the direction it faces, correspond to different areas of the body, the brain, and the emotions. They discovered that certain mudras lift the mood, while others calm the mind; some help us fall asleep, while others wake us up. One mudra can help with sinus problems, while another will affect digestion. According to Joseph and Lillian Le Page in their book, *Mudras for Healing and Transformation*, veteran yoga practitioners and founders of Integrative Yoga Therapy, "Mudras are a hidden treasure that open us to our own innate resources for healing at all levels of our being (Le Page & Le Page, 2012). In broad general terms, Western science agrees. "The hands' direct route to our motivation positive emotions, and cognitive abilities confirms their importance in our mental as well as our physical lives," wrote neuroscientist Kelly Lambert (2008, p. 69). But there are no randomized controlled trials of mudras.

If you think that the use of mudras to manage mood is an unproven, unscientific mystical theory, you're partly right. There's no research to date on the power of mudras alone to affect mood. However, in separate studies at the University of Pennsylvania, the

University of California, and one that is ongoing, Kirtan Kriya, as taught by the Kundalini master Yogi Bhajan, which includes mudras and mantras, was shown to increase short-term memory and cognitive function and to reduce stress (Khalsa, Amen, Hanks, Money, & Newberg, 2009; Newberg et al., 2010). Another protocol that uses both mudra and mantra, the LifeForce Chakra-Clearing Meditation (see pages 123–127), is currently being investigated. In this randomized controlled trial, the researchers are looking at psychotherapy with and without the mudra and mantra practice to examine its effect on depression.

If you are a person who needs to see the results of a randomized controlled trial before you introduce something new into your life or make a recommendation to a client, then skip this chapter. But the fact that it's not yet proven doesn't mean that it doesn't work. Try this simple exercise right now and I guarantee you will feel the breath being directed in your body. Simply sit with your hands in your lap and press the tips of your little fingers together. Take a few breaths through your nostrils and notice where you feel the breath in your body. Release the pressure on your little fingers and press your ring fingers together. Again, take a few breaths and notice where you feel the breath expanding in your body. Continue the same exercise with each finger and your thumbs. Then go back to your little finger again. Feel the difference? Try pressing all of your fingers and your thumbs together. Isn't it interesting? Most of us feel the breath move more deeply into the lungs when we press the little fingers together. We feel the breath move up through the torso as we move, finger by finger, from little finger to thumb. A small number of people feel the breath moving in reverse, but in my experience in leading this with thousands of people over the years, everyone feels the breath shift just by changing from one finger to another.

Still not convinced? Try this. Make a peace sign with both hands by folding the ring and pinky into the palm with your thumb on top and your index and middle fingers extended. Now bring

Figure 7.1. Happy Buddha Mudra

the sides of the index and middle fingers together so that they're touching. Bend your elbows and bring your arms on either side of your chest so that the fingers of both hands are pointing toward the sky (Figure 7.1). Sit for a few minutes, gazing from within at your brow point. You can add a mantra or prayer or an affirmation that feels authentic. Most people find that simply sitting with the mudra begins to lift the corners of the mouth and to restore a sense of well-being.

THE CALMING MUDRAS

As a way to calm and ground at the beginning of a session, psychologist Deborah Lubetkin uses Dhyana Mudra, with the right hand cradled in the left hand while touching the pads of the thumbs together (Figure 7.2). Simply doing the mudra yourself will help you sustain your own sense of ease in the face of the chaos that

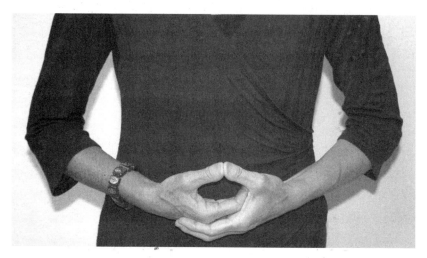

Figure 7.2. Dhyana Mudra

may be present in the treatment room. Even without instruction, your client may mirror your hand gesture. If she doesn't, you might invite her to try it, as you lead a simple breath, perhaps merely counting the beats of inhalation and exhalation, and then gradually extending the exhalation. In general, when the hands are facing downward, the gesture is more calming. Figures 7.3 through 7.5 illustrate a few other calming mudras.

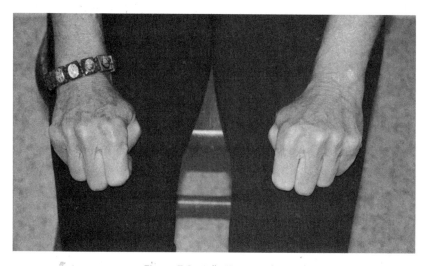

Figure 7.3. Adhi (First) Mudra

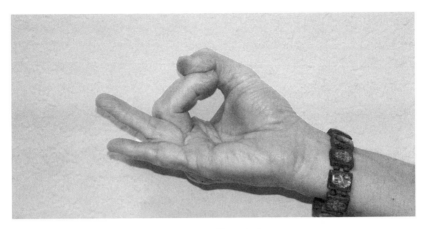

Figure 7.4. Chin Mudra

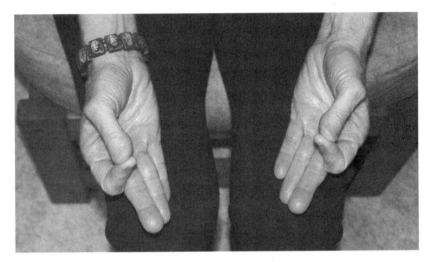

Figure 7.5. Chin Mudra in Lap

THE ENERGIZING MUDRAS

Energizing mudras can help when lethargy and depression are present. Simply sitting with Ganesha Mudra (Figure 7.6) straightens the spine, opens the chest, and invites more breath into the lungs. Gary had been a violin prodigy as a child, but when he was 14, the course of his life changed. Pain in his wrist and his neck made it difficult to play, and after years of devotion, opting out of sports and social activities with his peers in favor of practice, he gave up the instrument. He was grieving this momentous change in his life

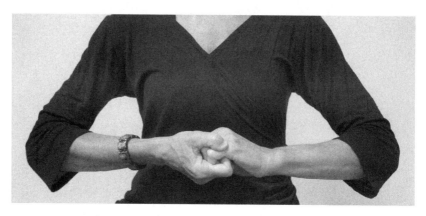

Figure 7.6. Ganesha Mudra

and felt isolated and alone at school. To add to his woes, his parents were in the midst of a rancorous divorce. Since team sports were not his thing, his therapist thought that a yoga practice might help him find more balance and carry him through this period of loss. He tried a group class at his mother's health club, but felt awkward and embarrassed and had trouble with the poses, so his therapist referred him to me.

At our initial meeting, before we moved to the yoga mat, he sat on my couch, shoulders slumped, a wrist brace on his right forearm. He said he didn't think he could do yoga because of his wrist, but his therapist had said that I taught yoga in a different way. I acknowledged that the Sun Salutations the teacher led at the health club must have been awkward and painful, because many of the poses in the sequence put pressure on his wrists. With modifications, he could certainly practice Sun Salutations, and he could do many other poses and yoga practices. While we continued to talk, I suggested that Gary and I both take Ganesha Mudra. As his fingers pulled against each other at his solar plexus, his spine automatically straightened and his breath deepened. I invited him to count his breath, suggesting that he inhale for four and exhale for four. We stopped talking and practiced the mudra for several minutes. When we released the mudra, Gary's eyes were brighter and he smiled for the first time in the session. "I think that helped my wrist," he said. He expressed optimism about what he might be able to accomplish. Six years later, Gary is in college, taking pre-med courses with the hope of becoming a doctor. He maintains a regular yoga practice and has a dream of using his medical training and yoga to serve youth in war-torn countries.

Figures 7.7 and 7.8 show two other stimulating mudras.

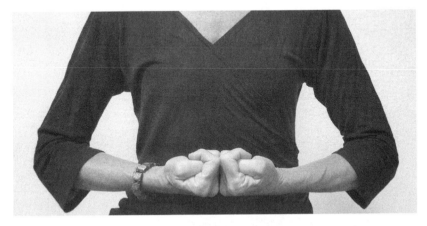

Figure 7.7. Brahma Mudra

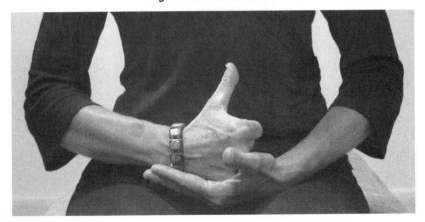

Figure 7.8. Shiva Linga Mudra

COMBINING MUDRA & MANTRA

Mudra is rarely practiced alone, but most often in combination with a pranayama breathing exercise, like those described in Chapters 4 and 5; with mantra, like those described in Chapter

6; with imagery, as described in Chapter 8; or to support meditation. In Chapter 8, on page 148, we use a hand gesture (drawing
the hands to the heart) with a mantra (so ham) and a visualization (an image for calm strength). There are infinite variations of
hand gestures and images and mantras and even affirmations that
can be practiced together, creating a synergistic effect that may
enhance the outcome of any one of the practices alone. "By combining mudras with affirmations, the gesture's essential meaning
is communicated directly to our body, mind, and spirit" (LePage,
2012). Several excellent resources for expanding your knowledge
of mudras and their therapeutic value are covered in Chapter 11.
Here, we will stick with the basic chakra tones covered in Chapter
6, pairing mudras with each tone to increase either the grounding
and lightly stimulating effect or the calming effect.

LIFEFORCE YOGA CHAKRA-CLEARING MEDITATIONS

What follows are two meditation practices that begin with two
breathing exercises you already know. Bellows Breath (Bhastrika)
clears the inner space with a stimulating practice that upon completion, as discussed in Chapter 5, kicks the parasympathetic nervous
system into gear. Bee Breath (Brahmari), as taught in Chapter 4, is
calming, and therefore balances the more stimulating effect of the
Bellows Breath. Following these breathing exercises, you and your
client can then practice the meditation that includes mantras and
mudras that are grounding and lightly energizing. Or you can choose
to do the more calming version. As a spacious and clear mind is the
result, either version of this practice can be a doorway into mindfulness meditation. These meditation practices are a portal into what T.
S. Eliot called "the still point in the turning world" (1943, p. 15). As
you practice or lead them, take time between each of the breathing
practices to sense the effects—the body sensations and the stillness
within—before moving into the mudra and mantra practice.

Figure 7.9. Deborah Lubetkin, PhD, teaching the LifeForce Yoga Clearing Meditation, Energizing Version to her client

LifeForce Yoga Chakra-Clearing Meditation: Energizing

The LifeForce Yoga Chakra-Clearing Meditation combines pranayama breathing, mantra chanting, and mudras that have been part of the lexicon of yoga for thousands of years. Based on my years of extensive personal practice and teaching, I have found that this particular pattern elevates mood for most people and is easy to learn and teach. This meditation is currently under scientific review in a clinical trial. Although we call this energizing, the effect of the mudras and tones, when practiced together, is more subtle than some of the more stimulating breathing practices. When one long tone is used for each chakra, rather than repeating the tone, the effect is more grounding. You and your clients will feel more present and alert after practice.

1. Practice one to three rounds of Bellows Breath (Bhastrika) to clear the space (see Chapter 5).
2. Practice three rounds of Bee Breath (Brahmari) on exhale only to calm the sympathetic nervous system, using the Shanmukhi Mudra or a modification to create sensory withdrawal (see Chapter 4).
3. With the mudras shown in Table 7.1, practice the specific mantra from the back of the throat, emphasizing the consonant: one long consonant with one long breath, closing the consonant with "mmm."
4. Lift the arms over the head, creating an open channel. Practice three times on three breaths, using each long breath to chant through all the tones.
5. Remaining with the arms over the head, inhale and interlace the fingers with the index finger extended. Hold the breath. On exhale with "ng" sound, float your arms down, palms open on your knees.
6. Upon completion, sit observing the effects. You may sit for as long as you wish in meditation, observing the breath or using your own meditation technique.

LifeForce Yoga Chakra-Clearing Meditation: Calming

The mudras in this version of the meditation deepen and calm the breath. The vowel sounds are more soothing. Many therapists teach this meditation to their anxious clients for home practice and also use it to begin a session. Of course, it's not a practice to introduce at the initiation of therapy. Rather, once there's a strong therapeutic

TABLE 7.1 LifeForce Yoga Chakra Clearing Meditation – Energizing

CHAKRA	MANTRA	MUDRA	ISSUE
Chakra 1 Muladhara (Base of spine)	Lum red	Hasta Mudra 1 Link the two little fingers together close to the base of the spine and pull. 	Attachment
Chakra 2 Svadhisthana (Low abdomen)	Vum orange	Hasta Mudra 2 Link the two ring fingers in front of the low abdomen and pull. 	Sexuality
Chakra 3 Manipura (Solar plexus)	Rum yellow	Hasta Mudra 3 Link the two middle fingers in front of the solar plexus and pull. 	Identity/ Self-Esteem
Chakra 4 Anahata (Heart)	Yum green	Dove (Kapota) Mudra Palms together as in prayer. Keep the base of the palms and the tips of the fingers together but cup the palms. 	Compassion/ Self-Acceptance

CHAKRA	MANTRA	MUDRA	ISSUE
Chakra 5 Vishuddha (Throat)	Hum blue	Lotus (Padma) Mudra Bring the hands together as in prayer. Keep the base of the palms, the little fingers and the thumbs together. Open all the other fingers wide like petals. 	Communication
Chakra 6 Ajna (Third Eye)	Om violet	Kali Mudra Clasp your hands together with hands cupped, hovering close to forehead without touching, and with your index finger extended forward horizontally. Elbows out to the sides. 	Mood
Chakra 7 Sahasrara (Crown of head)	Nnng white	Kali Mudra Clasp your hands together hovering above your crown with hands cupped, and extend your index finger vertically. Elbows out to the sides. 	Spirituality

alliance, you might invite your client to try something different to regulate the mood.

1. Practice three rounds of Bee Breath (Brahmari) on exhale only to calm the sympathetic nervous system, using the Shanmukhi Mudra or the modification to create sensory withdrawal (see Chapter 4).
2. With the mudras shown in Table 7.2, practice the calming tones mantras, giving each tone one long breath (see Chapter 6).
3. Hands remain in the lap in Dhyana Mudra, right nesting in left with thumbs touching. Practice three times on three breaths, using each long breath to chant through all the tones.
4. Upon completion, sit observing the effects. You may sit for as long as you wish in meditation, observing the breath or using your own meditation technique.

Application

Sue Dilsworth is a clinical psychologist and yoga therapist practicing in Allendale, Michigan, who uses both the calming and the energizing versions of this practice with her clients, depending on what mood is present. She teaches both versions of the chakra meditation to her clients, so that they can manage and balance their mood at home. Sue has a yoga therapy studio and a consultation room for psychotherapy. Although she keeps her practices separate, she teaches mudras and, in particular, the LifeForce Yoga Chakra-Clearing Meditation in both venues.

After a month of weekly treatment, Sue introduced the calming version to 40-year-old Darlene, a working professional who suffered a spinal cord injury in 1997 when she was thrown from a horse. The accident left her paralyzed from the middle of her thoracic spine down and struggling with depression ever since. She most often complains of feeling disconnected from others and often worries about being alone. Sue has helped Darlene foster a deeper connection to herself and others through the use of the

TABLE 7.2 LifeForce Yoga Chakra Clearing Meditation – Calming

CHAKRA	MANTRA	MUDRA	ISSUE
Chakra 1 Muladhara (Base of spine)	Ō as in go	Press the tips of the two little fingers together close to the base of the spine.	Attachment
Chakra 2 Svadhisthana (Low abdomen)	Ū as in you	Press the tips of the two ring fingers in front of the low abdomen.	Sexuality
Chakra 3 Manipura (Solar plexus)	Ah as in paw	Press the tips of the two middle fingers in front of the solar plexus.	Identity/ Self-Esteeem
Chakra 4 Anahata (Heart)	Ā as in pay	Dove (Kapota) Mudra Place hands together as in prayer in front of the heart, thumbs at the breast bone. Keep the base of the palms and the tips of the fingers together but cup the palms.	Compassion/ Self-Acceptance

Chakra 5 Vishuddha (Throat)	Ē as in tea	Lotus (Padma) Mudra Place hands together as in prayer, hovering in front of the throat. Keep the base of the palms, the little fingers and the thumbs together as you spread the other fingers wide like petals.	Communication
Chakra 6 Ajna (Third Eye)	Mmm	Anjali Mudra Bring the hands together into prayer positions, thumbs touching the bridge of the nose and the brow.	Mood
Chakra 7 Sahasrara (Crown of head)	Hnng	Dhyana Mudra Place the left hand in the lap, palm facing up. Place the right hand on top of the left with the palm facing up. Bring the tips of the thumbs to lightly touch.	Spirituality

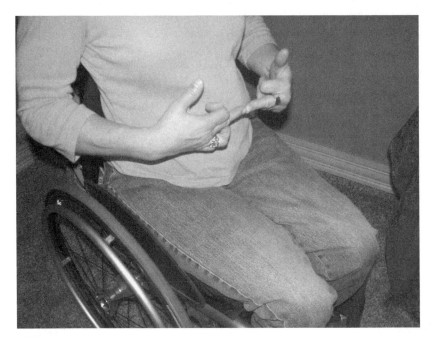

Figure 7.10. Dr. Sue Dilsworth's client, practicing the calming version of the LifeForce Yoga Chakra-Clearing Meditation

Chakra-Clearing Meditation (Tables 7.1 and 7.2) as well as yoga nidra (see Chapter 9), which means yogic sleep but is actually a form of meditation most often done in a supine position. After nearly 2 months of daily practice with the meditation and occasional practice of yoga nidra, Darlene's depressive symptoms lessened, and she began connecting socially with others again.

Mudras are most often integrated with other practices like breath awareness and mantras. Joy Bennett, a yoga therapist in Providence, Rhode Island, who shares an office with her psychiatrist husband Winn Bennett, has been working with a client named Bob for 3 years. She explains how she wove a mudra into their first session together:

> Bob is a 57-year-old municipal office worker for a large city who never married. He essentially likes the work he does, but finds it challenging to work with the new technology and security measures that his younger boss expects. By nature, he is an exceptionally meticulous and sensitive person and has difficulty being one of the

guys in a large office. He expressed fears about holding on to his job in what he described as an atmosphere of gossip, backstabbing, and a consistently high level of noise and chaos.

When he began working with me, he was suffering from migraines and insomnia, and had experienced two incidents of panic attacks. As he described these symptoms, his breathing was shallow, his shoulders were clenched, and his right foot and knee were jiggling up and down. The longer he talked about his problems on the job, the more visibly agitated he became—wiping his face with his hand, leaning back in his chair, and scratching the back of his head. So I asked him to ground his feet on the floor and feel the connection of his feet to the earth (he had removed his shoes for the session). Then I asked him to place one hand over his heart and one hand over his navel, and invited him to become aware of his breath. I offered him several ways to tap into this awareness: "Notice a gentle animation of the torso as you inhale and exhale." I paraphrased a line from the poet Rainer Maria Rilke: "Allow your breath to flow like a river, no forcing, and no holding back."

As his shoulders began to drop and his breath began to deepen, he told me that he was feeling some pressure and burning in his chest. I invited him to notice that sensation as we practiced Vajrapradama Mudra together (Figure 7.11). I interlaced my fingers, spread my thumbs, and dropped my elbows out to the side, and he mirrored the gesture. While we held the mudra, I gave him a brief description of the science of mudras and their particular energetic effect upon the body-mind. When I told him that this particular mudra would "cultivate a sense of unconditional trust and confidence within yourself so that you know you have what you need to manage your life," he was visibly moved. He closed his eyes and sat up straighter in his chair, elongating his spine. I explained to him that we were holding the mudra for a little while longer, so that the energetic effect could imprint itself within the body. I invited him to slowly bring the effect of Vajrapradama Mudra to the pressure in his chest, like a camera adjusting a lens into focus, soothing

Figure 7.11. Joy Bennett, LFYP-2, leading Vajrapradama Mudra with client.

the burning sensation in the heart space. Though his eyes remained closed, a large tear rolled down one cheek. His facial features began to soften, his jaw relaxed, and his lips parted slightly.

I asked Bob if he could create an intention for his session that day—perhaps a single word or a simple phrase arising of its own accord. He said he was visualizing the word *peace* on his heart, that more than anything, he wanted peace in his life.

I guided Bob to release the mudra with a deep inhalation as he extended his arms outward, then upward over his head into Mountain Breath, offering his intention skyward. I instructed him to release the posture when his exhalation arrived, floating his arms and hands down to his sides. We practiced this together three times to seal his intention and then continued with his session.

Since that first session 3 years ago, Bob has returned for 32 more sessions and has made progress in dealing with his anxiety. His breathing has deepened, and he has developed a repertoire of his favorite calming poses, such as Seated Forward Fold and Child Pose. He recently moved to a larger apartment and has created a yoga room out of the second bedroom. Bob practices before work in the morning and has found that he is more grounded and less reactive to the challenges of his work day. He purchased an iPod for himself to download the classical music that he enjoys, and is finding that he is capable of learning "all that new technology."

It sometimes amazes me how the most ostensibly conservative or strait-laced clients can often embrace the more seemingly esoteric practices like bee breath or bija mantras or mudras. Again and again, I've observed that when the therapist is comfortable with the practice because she's experienced the effects herself and she conveys that knowledge and enthusiasm, her clients will find the benefits of the practice for themselves.

CHAPTER 8

THE YOGA OF IMAGERY (Bhavana) & AFFIRMATION (Sankalpa)

In yoga, we call an image or vision that inspires us a *bhavana*. Yogis have used imagery as well as affirmation, called *sankalpa*, for thousands of years to balance extreme states of mind and emotion. Both visual imagery and affirmation (which includes, as a first step, setting an intention) have also been important components in some forms of psychotherapy. In looking at imagery and affirmation from a yoga perspective, you may find some techniques that are useful to you and your clients. Let's take a look at imagery first.

WHY WORK WITH IMAGERY?

Imagery speaks to our earliest memories and perceptions of the world. Before we had language, we thought in pictures. The more primitive areas of the brain process pictures, perceptions, and feelings. If trauma and loss occurred before we had language or in our earliest attempts to talk, it makes sense that imagery, which bypasses the language areas of the brain, should be integrated into therapeutic treatment. No matter our age, if we are involved in a traumatizing event, the increased cortisol that floods our brains makes linear thinking impossible. During such an event, our memories are stored incoherently and are fraught with emotion. These are known as implicit memories and are not chronological, but rather body-based. Implicit memory manifests as body sensations and emotional surges. According to psychologist Belleruth Naparstek, author of *Invisible Heroes: Survivors of Trauma and How They Heal*, "Trauma produces changes in the brain that impede a person's ability to think and talk about the event but that actually accentuate their capacity for imaging and emotional-sensory experiencing around it. . . . Imagery uses what's most accessible in the traumatized brain to help with the healing" (2004, p. 13).

Whether your client is suffering from PTSD, in the throes of a panic attack, or burdened by depression, imagery can serve to moderate the symptoms and bring her back into balance. We can teach clients to tap into their brain's capacity for picture making to help them regulate their emotions. An image that is soothing can calm an agitated mind, while an image of strength can offer a personal sense of power. An image of a loved one can be a tool to self-soothe. For example, even if we've had a rough start, most of us have a memory of a being who affirmed us. It may have been a grandparent or another relative, or a beloved four-legged companion who wagged his tail in abundant joy when we entered the room. Had no one been there, the failure to thrive would have done us in long ago. By evoking that image of an affirming being, we are creating fertile ground for contentment to grow.

INTRODUCING IMAGERY IN A SESSION

I have found that most people are eager to close their eyes and think of an image. You might begin with a question like, "Would you like to find an image that is soothing for those times when you feel stressed?" When your client agrees, you need not even ask her to close her eyes. When you simply suggest that she think of an image that is peaceful and serene, she will likely close her eyes. If she doesn't, there may be a very good reason, which can be the basis for a deeper inquiry. Is she feeling unsafe in the session? If so, what might help her to feel safer with you? If there's no good reason, then you can suggest that it's easier to find an image if her eyes are closed. If she has trouble finding an image, then validate that. Ask her if she might be willing to simply think the word *peace*. Check in with your client afterward to see if an image arose. If not, there's another jumping off point for a deeper inquiry.

Adding Affirmation

Imagery works hand in hand with affirmation. If your client arrives in an agitated state with racing thoughts, you might invite him to join you in a calming breath from Chapter 4, and then ask him to imagine a place where he might feel peaceful and serene. Once an image is established that evokes a calm state of mind, it is easy to guide a client into setting an intention or positive resolve. For example, I might say to a client or a class: "From this place of peace, invite a heartfelt prayer or an intention to reveal itself." You can further develop the client's intention or prayer into an affirmation. In the discussion that follows the exercise, invite your client to share the intention and then help him frame it in the present tense. For example, "May I be centered and find balance" can be transformed into an affirmation like "I am centered and in balance." "I want clarity" can become "Clarity breathes through me now."

When we can guide the client to find her intention for herself, rather than suggesting one, the result is a more authentic intention, out of which a more self-empowering affirmation emerges. The mind will resist an intention that feels imposed from outside. Current research suggests that if your client arrives agitated and angry, without laying the groundwork through the use of a breathing technique and the evocation of imagery, saying "I am peaceful" may have just the opposite effect. Researchers at the University of Waterloo found that participants with low self-esteem felt worse after repeating the positive affirmation, "I am a lovable person," multiple times (Wood, 2009).

Application

Cindy Naughton, a counselor and life coach in Ventura, California, worked with Patrice, a graduate student and athlete in her early 20s who was enrolled in a highly competitive PhD program. Patrice had a history of anxiety and perfectionism and bouts of depression that were now exacerbated by her academic program and her current inability to exercise because of a sports injury. She entered Cindy's office complaining of obsessive thoughts and, most troubling to her, compulsive eating during her prolonged recovery from a torn Achilles tendon. During their first session, Cindy invited Patrice to close her eyes and practice Yogic Three-Part Breath (described in Chapter 4) and then invited her to recall a time when she felt peaceful and safe in nature. When Patrice shared a memory of one of her favorite visits to the water, Cindy encouraged her to describe the experience with all five of her senses.

Cindy has bolsters and cushions in her office. Once Patrice had calmly described a scene on the beach and the light off the surface of the ocean, Cindy supported her client into a reclined position and asked her to notice her normal breathing pattern. When Patrice was comfortable in the position, Cindy guided her in Ocean-Sounding Victory Breath (Chapter 4) as she recalled her soothing ocean image. When Patrice said that she never felt this relaxed in her daily life, Cindy asked if she would like to create an affirmation about feeling more relaxed. She agreed and, with Cindy's coaching, affirmed "peace breathes through me now." After Patrice's direct experience of feeling relaxed, Cindy helped her set "stepping stones" of practices to support her intention to sustain relaxation in her everyday life. Together they discussed her schedule and her home environment to decide what practices were realistic in the time she had early in the morning and late in the afternoon. They came up with a plan of gradually increasing time periods of practice that Patrice thought she could manage.

Social worker, addictions specialist, and yoga teacher Kathryn Shafer, who practices in Jupiter, Florida, helped her anxious client

Angela transform a calming image into an experience of self-soothing. An experienced yoga teacher, Angela was having trouble setting boundaries and caring for herself. Angela controlled her anxiety by managing the world around her and caretaking for others. She expressed her struggle to give herself permission to let go and relax. When Kathryn asked her if there was a word, phrase, or sound that could express what she wanted, she began to sing a popular song by Cyndi Lauper, "Girls Just Want to Have Fun." Kathryn invited her to stand and shake her body as they sang the chorus together. Then Kathryn helped her ground the awakened energy and sense of fun in a Standing Mountain posture, from which she invited Angela to breathe and center. With eyes closed, Angela found her affirmation: "I am relaxed and love the fun I am having now." Kathryn continued the theme of fun as she led several rounds of Breath of Joy, as described in Chapter 5. As she sensed her body after the breathing practice, Angela said she was hearing the soothing sound of water.

As the session progressed, Kathryn supported Angela in a restorative pose on her back, with props for her shoulders, knees, and neck. As a yoga teacher and psychotherapist, like Cindy in Ventura, Kathryn has props in her office, so inviting a client to lie down on the floor is easy. You may have a treatment room with a couch and a chair or two, where lying down might not be an option. You can still do the imagery and affirmation work, and suggest that your client take her soothing image and new affirmation with her to a restorative yoga class, or onto her yoga mat at home, or in bed in the morning.

Once in the restorative pose, Kathryn led Angela in an Ocean-Sounding Victory Breath (Chapter 4) and invited her to return to the soothing sound of water. Angela's image for fun was "swimming in the water with the fish." As Angela's breathing became more regular, Kathryn invited her to give herself permission to let go more deeply by inhaling the word *let* and exhaling the word *go*. "Notice how much deeper you can relax," Kathryn said, "and listen to the water. See the fish swimming in the cool clear calm water . . . letting everything relax." Before Kathryn led Angela to transition out of the pose, she invited her to try the soothing sound "mmm," for the brow point, the place where we often feel the effects of anxiety and depression most directly. In yoga tradition the brow point is the seat of wisdom and intuition, and we can soothe it with a sound like "mmm" or brighten it with a visual image of light.

Modifications

When using imagery, it's important to allow for the possibility that your client will not have access to an image. Psychiatrist Francoise Adan, medical director of the University Hospitals Connor Integrative Medicine Network in Cleveland, normalizes whatever her patient expresses in this regard. While she encourages her patient to use all her senses and asks if there's an image or a memory that arises, Francoise normalizes the experience for someone for whom no sensory details or images arise by saying, "It's fine if nothing comes up, but just check in." She says that usually patients are surprised by what does arise.

In my own work with clients, I cue to imagery without providing it directly. For example, I may say, "Perhaps it's an image from nature where you could imagine feeling calm, or a memory of a time when you felt peaceful and serene." I want the client to draw his image from his own life experience, so I resist the impulse to make my suggestion too concrete by, for example, suggesting the image of a still pond or a meadow. I also want to normalize the inability to find an image, so I will say, "Some of us think in words and sounds, so if that's you, simply think the word *peace* or imagine a soothing tone."

Images can be used to help foster the client's goal in therapy, even when a positive image evokes painful feelings. The very discovery that conflicted feelings are associated with the positive image can be useful in the therapeutic process. For example, Francoise Adan worked with an overweight patient named Jenny who expressed the wish to lose weight. She guided Jenny to close her eyes and imagine an image of herself at her ideal weight. She then asked Jenny to sense the feelings and sensations in her body that this image of herself evoked. Jenny was surprised to realize that the image of herself at her ideal weight brought up overwhelming feelings of fear and anxiety. This powerful insight allowed Jenny to understand how she might be sabotaging her own best efforts to lose weight so as to avoid those uncomfortable feelings.

When Francoise affirmed Jenny's inner protector by agreeing, "It makes sense that you would want to avoid feeling overwhelmed and afraid," Jenny could relax and be more accepting of her behavior. Such insight, culled from imagery, can go a long way in helping clients begin to make small, manageable changes, rather than big radical ones, like drastic diets that have not worked in the past. After realizing why the big steps like a popular new diet that seemed to work for everyone else didn't work for her, a client will be more open to a suggestion of a baby step. Francoise might ask her patient, "What is the smallest possible thing you could do today to move you toward your goal?" It could be something as simple as eating two pieces of bread with dinner instead of three. "That's fantastic," Francoise will say. "Do you think you could try that?"

Had Francoise not asked Jenny to close her eyes and imagine herself at her ideal weight, Jenny might not have discovered the pattern of self-sabotaging behavior herself. By inviting her patient to imagine herself at the weight she wanted to be, Francoise helped her discover the block to making the change. Once there was awareness of the obstacle, her patient could begin to challenge it in small ways.

An image is like a destination point on the map. You need to pinpoint your destination to get there. In my own work, I like to let clients know that they have all the tools they need inside to reach that destination.

Contraindications

For clients who present with symptoms of dissociation, or visual or auditory hallucinations, imagery may take them farther from reality.

In such cases, you might lead a breathing practice with eyes opened and focused on a pleasant object in the room. After that, you can encourage your client to notice the feeling in the areas of the body that have a lot of nerve endings, and therefore a lot of sensation, like the lips, palms, fingertips, or feet. Cueing to direct sensation in specific body parts, rather than a more global awareness of sensation, is best when working with clients who tend to dissociate.

AFFIRMATION: ARISING FROM WITHIN THE CLIENT

After I've led a brief centering that includes an intention for our work together, I check in with my client, asking him if he would be willing to share his intention. From there, we reframe the intention to be in the present tense, and this becomes the client's affirmation. I've never heard anyone say that he was unwilling to share his intention, but quite a few have told me that they couldn't come up with one. I welcome this opportunity to dive deeper—is the mind too busy, jumping from idea to idea (indicating an underlying anxious state of mind (*rajasic*), or is it blank, which would indicate an underlying depressed state of mind (*tamasic*)? This gives me a good idea of where to begin, and I can offer a breath or a mudra to bring more balance into the presenting mood. After a brief breathing practice, I might ask if it makes sense to the client to breathe serenity through a narrow channel of his jumpy mind. If, on the other hand, he is feeling depressed, I might ask if it feels authentic to imagine breathing energy and light through the heaviness he may be feeling.

Francoise helps her patients find their own affirmations, first by giving them an example. "I tell them that I personally find the words *I am* to be very powerful." Then she leads a simple meditation. She shares an example of her own and invites them to breathe it in and out along with her: "I am peaceful and present." And then when they seem relaxed, she will ask them to open their hearts to why they are there—"What is the gift you would like to give to yourself?" Then, as she did with Jenny, she might ask them to sense what they feel as they imagine that outcome. Next, she invites them to put that feeling into a sentence or a phrase, using "I am" as a start. "Often patients cry when they say it out loud," she says, as in "I, Susan, am confident and clear." When clients hear their self-created affirmation repeated back three times, as in "You, Susan, are confident and clear," by their therapist, or a small group or a partner in a workshop, the experience is often profoundly moving and empowering.

Sometimes using "I am" might feel inauthentic to your client. For example, if your client is feeling revved up and anxious, breathing the words "I am peaceful" might evoke feelings of annoyance or even anger. If the state of mind isn't addressed first through breath or imagery, the affirmation might seem false. If the mind is agitated even after using the breathing practices described in Chapter 4, ask your client if she can breathe a small channel of peace through the chaos. Perhaps she will feel comfortable with "Peace breathes through me now," which allows her to acknowledge the chaos. It's a baby step, but it's a start.

Here are some other examples:

1. I am clear and focused.
2. Clarity flows through me now.
3. I accept myself as I am.
4. Acceptance flows through me now.
5. I am loving and lovable.
6. Love breathes through me now.

One way to introduce an affirmation, imagery practice, or a body-sensing practice is to acknowledge the client's possible discomfort. "This might sound bizarre," Francoise might say to the woman who is overweight, "but just play along with me for a moment. If you're comfortable, close your eyes and sense into how it feels in your body to be carrying more weight than you want." When framed this way, the client is given permission to "play along" or not, to close eyes or not, and in general this allows for a greater sense of comfort with whatever new practice is being suggested.

Affirmation With Trauma Victims

Jaime Hedlund is a yoga therapist who with Mark Lilly, Street Yoga Founder, and social worker Erin O'Reilly designed and implemented a yoga-based protocol for helping young people recover from the trauma of sexual abuse at Morrison's Family Sexual Abuse Treatment Program in Portland, Oregon. The Healing Childhood Sexual Abuse With Yoga (HCSAY) Program uses specially designed integrative and therapeutic yoga practices to help heal the trauma of childhood sexual abuse. The program spans two 8-week sessions and works with two different age groups: teens first, who are trained as Teen Leaders. In the second session, the Teen Leaders assist and mentor preteen girls. Jaime feels that the second session has been the most transformative for the teens.

At the heart of this program is the desire to create safety, build assertiveness, and reduce the chances that the girls will be revictimized. The students are taught mantra-like affirmations as a way to "rebuild healthy vocabularies—the way they think about, feel, and live in their bodies and minds," says Jaime. "Our great hope is for the girls to create and restore for themselves a compassionate inner voice that shapes a greater sense of self-worth and compassion. From that place of inner strength, the girls can start to go outward, building healthy relationships with friends, family, and their communities."

A sexual trauma survivor with developmental trauma may come to therapy with such strong feelings of self-blame that finding positive messages to say to herself feels impossible. If a client is currently or has recently been living in an abusive situation, there may be no context for framing a positive affirmation in the present tense. Although she may need help in shifting from self-blame to self-talk that is kind and compassionate, she may also resist your suggestion of a positive affirmation because it feels phony or inauthentic.

Figure 8.1. Creating safe and sacred space in the Healing Childhood Sexual Abuse with Yoga Program in Portland, Oregon

However, including an affirmation in a yoga program like HCSAY or in a simple pose in your office with feet grounded, like the Seated Mountain with integrity that Joe Walter used in Chapter 4, can create a felt sense of strength in which an affirmation that you provide feels more authentic and acceptable. In this case and in other situations when working with teens and children, suggesting affirmations—such as "I am strong," "Strength breathes through me," "I am confident," or "Confidence breathes through me"—in the context of yoga is appropriate. With the teens and young girls in the HCSAY program, mantralike affirmations are offered within yoga poses.

Jaime describes the power of affirmation in the context of the teen leader–young girl relationship. "At the beginning of each session before the young girls come into the room, we have a moment of centering with the teens. There is usually a lot of nervous energy among them. In the beginning, the teens believed that the little girls would hate them, be mean to them, or not be appreciative of the session. So, in these precious moments of centering, we ask that the teens close their eyes, focus on their breath, and repeat to themselves, "I am wise, beautiful, and have so much goodness to give and receive. I am here to do my best."

Once the young girls enter, the class forms a circle and begins with a group check-in (Figure 8.1). Each girl creates a movement and chants an affirmation in line with the class theme, which the group repeats back. For example, a girl might say, "I am Judy, and I am strong." Everyone copies Judy's movement and repeats, "Judy is strong!" Other examples from the HCSAY class: "I am Judy, and I trust myself." Everyone repeats: "Judy trusts herself!" "I am Judy and I have the right to personal space." Everyone repeats: "Judy has the right to personal space!"

The mantra-like affirmations Jaime and her colleagues introduce in the class are a means of rebuilding a sense of safety and trust in praise from others. Praise is complicated for childhood victims of sexual abuse and can often bring up distrust and fear. For many, compliments were the means by which the abuser groomed the victim. Even adult survivors of sexual abuse may numb out when praised. Says Jaime, "kind words coming from the entire group of peers, trusted teens, and staff, in an environment that was not a threat to safety, allowed the girls to hear and start to believe them."

At the end of the class, each teen stands in front of the younger girl she is mentoring and, while looking into the younger girl's eyes and offering her that week's handout, repeats her affirmation. Through the process of the program, the teens become more self-aware and report feelings of greater compassion for themselves. They see themselves as wise leaders with something real and helpful to offer. "At the end," says Jaime, "they were grateful to be a part of something special for the little girls, so the younger ones didn't have to suffer in the same way that they had."

Affirmation in Recovery

Whether you call it community, fellowship, or *sangha*, the support of one's peers is an important element in achieving and sustaining recovery from substance abuse. A yoga class or 12-step meeting or group therapy for those in recovery are all venues well suited for the practice of affirmation and imagery. In any of these settings, after leading a centering exercise in which the formulation of intention is included, you can invite the individuals in the group to inhale their intention, in the present tense, into the heart, and to exhale out whatever is blocking the full manifestation of that intention in their lives. Or you can ask the group to say each person's intention back, as Jaime did with the girls in Oregon. Or you can invite imagery and affirmation into yoga poses, as Ann Friedenheim, the substance abuse counselor and yoga teacher we met in Chapter 3, does in her yoga classes for recovery for folks in residential treatment facilities, a therapeutic community, and a halfway home. If you don't teach yoga, you can simply ask the group to stand and take a posture or gesture that embodies their intention. They can use their imaginations, because there is no wrong way to do this. This can become a fun exercise that bonds the group, as you go around the room, letting each person demonstrate the pose or gesture they associate with their intention as they verbalize it with a word or a phrase. Then lead the rest of the group in mirroring each individual's gesture and verbal intention.

Understanding that affirmations take on more power when embodied in a pose, Ann uses postures to cultivate them. In a typical class, she might lead participants through a breathing exercise like Pulling Prana, as described in Chapter 5. In one particular class, Ann invited participants into a wide-legged stance. As they inhaled, they stood with arms upraised, legs straight. On the exhale, they bent knees and brought arms into cactus position in a wide-legged squat known as the Victory Goddess Pose (Figure 8.2). They practiced without an affirmation and then paused. In the pause, as Ann cued them to feel the sensations in their hands and feet, as a way of grounding that sense of presence evoked by the repetition of the pose and pranayama breathing, she also invited her students to think of a quality that they wished to cultivate in their recovery process. "People chose determination, open mindedness, pacing, wisdom, patience, learning to take direction, and staying calm in the midst of uncertainty." Ann used imagery, guiding her students

Figure 8.2. Victory Goddess Pose

to imagine that the quality they had chosen surrounded them. As they inhaled, she guided them to reach up to connect with this quality. As they exhaled into the bent-knee position, this time she guided them to bring their hands to their hearts, drawing the quality within them with each breath.

Affirmation & Spirituality

Finding the doorway for your client into the use of affirmation or prayer is important. It may be that the portal is through the client's belief system. Joy Bennett, a yoga therapist in Providence, Rhode Island, worked with Catherine, a 50-year-old immigrant from Eastern Europe with a deep love for her Catholic heritage and a regular prayer life. When she entered yoga therapy she was suffering from frequent crying jags, panic attacks, and expressed feelings of hopelessness. Her shoulders were rounded and she could not stand up straight. She was open to learning more about the principles of yoga and felt comfortable with many of the practices, yet it became apparent after a few sessions that she wanted to integrate the Eastern practices of yoga with her more traditional Catholic faith.

Joy comes from a Catholic background and was able to draw upon different prayers that could be incorporated with breath and asanas. One day, Catherine was feeling overwhelmed, exhibiting physical indications of both anxiety (shallow breath) and depression (rounded shoulders). As they sat together in straight-backed chairs, Joy guided Catherine to lengthen her spine one vertebra at a time and to place her hands, palms up, in her lap. Joy invited her to close her hands, curling her fingers toward the palms on the out breath, then inviting her to open her hands on the in breath. They continued in this manner for several rounds of breath (closing hands on the exhale, opening the hands on the inhale) as Joy invited Catherine to match the movement of her hands with the movement of her breath (Figure 8.3). As she was doing so, Joy spoke of surrendering to the mystery of God, deeply present within her. "The image of letting go, and of surrender to God's plan for her was of great value to Catherine," Joy says. Joy noticed that her hand movements (and her breath) began to deepen and slow down. On an inhalation, Joy invited her to keep the hands open, in stillness, as she continued to breathe normally, as Joy recited the prayer of St. Ignatius of Loyola.

"The openness of her hands became an offering," Joy says, "a personification of these words, and tears began to flow from Catherine's closed eyes, as her head nodded in a yes motion." Joy continued to repeat parts of this prayer throughout her session, moving through a series of poses on the mat, as in the complete expression of Mountain Pose, arms extended, as well as in the surrender of a forward bend. "This was of great value to her as she embodied her poses completely, with the words of St. Ignatius resonating within her."

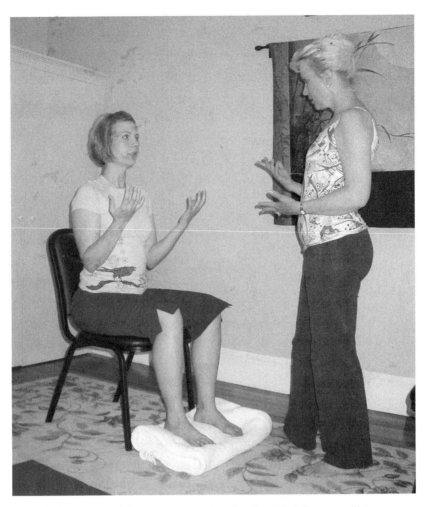

Figure 8.3. Joy Bennett, LFYP-2, meeting the client's belief system with prayer

PRACTICES

I've included two practice scripts in this chapter that use imagery and affirmation. The bhavana guided imagery practice can also be found on CD (see Chapter 11).

Practice: Bhavana—Calm Strength Image

I've included this practice which I also guide on a CD (see Chapter 11) so that you might have a script to practice leading a guided imagery bhavana with your clients. This bhavana exercise for calm strength also uses pranayama breathing and mantra. You may wish to use it in your office as a way of fostering self-efficacy in a client or helping her maintain steadiness through a difficult time. Or you may lead it in a group or workshop setting. It can be used for every diagnostic category, except where there may be a tendency to hallucinate.

First, after leading a calming breath, ask your client to think of an image that evokes a sense of calm strength in her heart and mind. Next, ask your client to share that image with you. If she had trouble finding an image, you might invite her to see the words "calm strength" or "courage," as described above. Once you are assured that your client has a suitable image, invite her to close her eyes.

The following is an example of how I would lead this practice.

SETUP SCRIPT

We'll be using a 4:4:6 breath, exhaling with a mantra. This means that you'll be breathing in for four counts, holding the breath for four counts, and then breathing out for six counts. But you don't need to count the exhalation, because we'll be releasing the breath with the mantra "so ham," which means "I am that." In using the mantra "so ham," you're saying that on the deepest level, beneath all the obstructions—the chronic tension in your physical body, or feelings like fear and sadness in your emotional body, or the negative self-talk that might be going on in your mental body—there is no separation between you and that image for calm strength that you are holding in your heart. Beneath the blocks and obstructions, you already are that. The seeds for your well-being are already planted. We just need to choose to water those seeds, seeds like calm strength and peace and love, rather than the seeds of self-hatred and judgment.

Come into a comfortable seated position with your spine erect. Allow your eyes to close and begin noticing the breath as it moves in and out through the tip of your nostrils. No need to alter or change your breathing pattern. Just notice.

Now bring into your mind's heart an image for calm strength. It may be an image from nature . . . or a face . . . or a symbol. Some of us are more auditory than visual, or we're more kinesthetic. If that's you and no image readily appears, then just think the words "calm strength."

Now see that image for calm strength or think the words "calm strength." As you breathe in for four counts, you will be extending your arms out in front of your solar plexus, the manipura chakra, which is your seat of identity and self-esteem. Then you hold the breath for four counts, visualizing your image for calm strength or thinking the words. Next you will draw your hands to your solar plexus, one palm folded on top of the other, with the mantra "so ham." We'll repeat this three times, and then we'll do the gesture and mantra one more time, drawing calm strength to the heart.

Find your comfortable and steady seat and allow your eyes to close. Inhale your arms out in front of your solar plexus. Hold the breath, 2, 3, 4, visualizing your image for calm strength. Exhale with "soooo hammm."

Inhale, 2, 3, 4.

Hold the breath, embracing your image.

Exhale soooo hammm.

Inhale, 2, 3, 4.

Hold the breath with your image for calm strength in your heart's mind. Exhale with soooo hammm.

Now, on this last round, draw your image for calm strength into your heart. Inhale, 2, 3, 4.

Hold the breath. I am that.

Sooo hammm.

When you complete, sit with your eyes closed with your image for calm strength, feeling the shift in your posture, your breath, and your general well-being.

After leading this bhavana, check in with your client. How does he feel? When might he find this practice useful at home?

LifeForce Yoga Bhavana: Say Yes to Yourself

I have led this bhavana in mood management workshops and with individual clients. A full version is available on CD (see Chapter 11). Most people find the memory or imagination of a supportive being comforting. It also helps clients gain clarity about their future by allowing them to remember what kinds of activities have been most gratifying in the past. This exercise can help clients make decisions about a future course of action or a major change in their lives.

Setup is crucial in helping your clients envision a being (two-legged, four-legged, winged, real, or imagined) who can indeed say yes to them. Some will have trouble coming up with a being in their childhood, so it's important to allow them to imagine a being from any time in their lives, including a deity. Also, some people can feel triggered by the mention of a particular age when something difficult may have happened to them. The language in the setup is important in that it needs to encourage participants to release an old story should one arise. In bold are the two important points your client should understand before you begin.

SETUP SCRIPT

In this guided visualization practice, you're going to see yourself at different ages in your life doing something you loved. Then you're going to imagine a being coming into the place where you are totally absorbed in what you are doing and you will be invited to feel that being's deep and acknowledging yes.

Someone in your life has said yes to you, or you wouldn't be here with me now. Someone has seen and acknowledged the person you are. It may have been a grandparent or another relative. Perhaps it was a teacher, a therapist, a lover, or a friend. It may even have been a friend in the animal kingdom.

I know there have been "yeses" in your life, because infants in orphanages after both world wars, who did not receive any kind of yes, any holding or care other than a strict adherence to hygiene, failed to gain weight and develop properly. Many of them died. And you are here on the planet in this body you've been given. You may not have had an easy life, and like many of us, you may not have received all the love you needed when you needed it most. But somewhere along the line, someone has cared. You didn't have to do anything. You didn't have to prove yourself.

Just your very being on the earth, the fact of your existence, was enough. You were seen, acknowledged, appreciated, and loved.

If there have been a lot of "no's" in your life, it may be hard to remember the "yeses." Or if one of the people who said yes to you also hurt you in some way, rather than imagining that person in this exercise, think of another being—perhaps the devoted eyes of an animal you have known or a deity or spirit guide.

In "Yes to Yourself," you're going to be visualizing snapshots of your life, looking at imaginary pictures of you at various ages. **If I happen to mention an age when something painful happened to you, don't get stuck there. Flip the album page to the next year. Or think about something positive that happened that year.** Just because that awful thing may have happened when you were 7, doesn't mean there weren't times that year when you laughed. At each age I mention there will be a moment when I invite you to imagine a being coming into the space where you are. **This being need not have existed in your life at that particular age. In fact, for most of us, there was no such being as a constant companion who could really see us for who we were. Feel free to bring in a being from another time in your life, or an angel or spirit guide.** The good news is that our brains are malleable. If you are carrying your story of not being seen or not receiving the love you needed when you needed it around with you and it is causing you to suffer, this is an opportunity to rewire those neuronal pathways and to give yourself, through the guidance of my voice, what you need to create a new story.

LIFEFORCE YOGA BHAVANA: YES TO YOURSELF SCRIPT

Make any small adjustments to your position, either lying on your back or sitting in a chair, to make yourself as comfortable as possible.

Inhale and tighten your gluteus muscles, make fists, squinch up your face. Squeeze the last vestiges of tension, whatever is blocking you from the free flow of your open heart and clear mind. Exhale and let it go completely. Let the tension dissolve into the earth.

Find an even and steady breath, perhaps four or five beats in and four or five beats out.

Now bring into your heart's mind an image of a being who has said yes to you. It might be a grandparent or a teacher or a therapist. It might be a friend from the animal kingdom. It could be a deity. Feel that being's benevolent regard. Feel that being's yes.

Now, imagine that you've found a dusty old photo album with your name on it. See it in your mind's eye. It doesn't matter that such a document of your childhood may never have existed; imagine it now.

Open your album. See a picture of you as the bright shining baby you were. See your radiance.

Now turn the pages through your baby pictures to a picture of yourself at 3 years old. See yourself doing something you loved to do when you were 3—maybe running around your yard, or dressing your doll, or playing with blocks or another favorite toy, or drawing, or dancing around the living room. See yourself so absorbed in your play that nothing else in your life matters to you.

Now see a benevolent being coming into the space where you are playing. Maybe this being enters from another time in your life. Maybe it's your dog or your spirit guide. See this being's face light up with pleasure at the sight of you so happy, so fulfilled. Imagine this being laughing with delight, clapping hands, saying yes to the amazing child you are. (Pause.)

It doesn't matter that this may have rarely or never happened. Imagine it now.

Now turn the pages of your photo album through your childhood years to a picture of yourself when you were 9 years old. See yourself doing something you loved—swimming, riding your bike, reading, drawing, climbing a tree, swinging on a swing, whatever it was you might have been doing when you were 9 that totally absorbed your mind and spirit. See yourself fully engaged in your play. You at 9, doing something so engaging that you forgot other things, or didn't even hear your name being called for dinner.

Now see that benevolent being coming into the space where you are playing. See this being's face light up with pleasure at the sight of you so happy, so fulfilled. Imagine this being saying a big yes to you and really meaning it. It doesn't matter that this may rarely or never have happened. Imagine it now.

Continue flipping the pages of your album through your adolescence until you come to a picture of yourself at 16. What were you doing at 16 that made you forget about everything else in your life, that brought you totally present to the experience of the moment? See yourself doing that one thing that so absorbed your mind and spirit that you forgot your troubles. Now see that benevolent being coming into the space where you are playing or studying or writing or singing or sewing. See this being's face light up with pleasure at the sight of you so present, so fulfilled. Imagine that this being says yes to you, to the precious teenager you are. It doesn't matter that this may rarely or never have happened. Imagine it now.

Now turn the pages of your album until you find a picture of yourself in your 20s, so absorbed in your work or your play that you forgot about everything else—maybe holding a baby, maybe solving a problem, maybe writing or reading or running or making art. Whatever it was, see yourself doing that one thing now. Then imagine that your benevolent being comes into the place where you are so connected, so present. See this being's face light up with pleasure at the sight of your absolute fulfillment in this moment. Feel this being's joy in seeing and acknowledging the creative and beautiful adult you are. Hear this being's big yes. It doesn't matter that this may rarely or never have happened. Imagine it now.

Keep turning, flipping through the decades of your life.

Now, turn to a recent picture of yourself, perhaps in the last 6 months; any time in the recent past when you were doing something that totally absorbed your mind and spirit. Dancing, loving, reading, painting, writing, running, practicing yoga. See yourself doing that thing now that takes you beyond happiness, beyond sadness, to a place where you are connected, where your mind and body and spirit are one. Now see your benevolent being entering the place where you are so connected, so present. See this being's face light up with pleasure at the sight of you so utterly fulfilled. Feel this being's joy in seeing and acknowledging the creative and beautiful adult you are. Feel this being's yes. See this being laughing with delight, clapping hands, saying, "Yes!"

Now say yes to yourself. Give yourself permission to play, to love what you're doing without doubt or fear. Say, "Yes, this is good. There's a time for this timelessness, this spaciousness in my life."

Now imagine yourself looking down at your physical body sitting in a chair or lying on the earth. Look with compassion at this body that has held you through all these years, and say yes to yourself.

Now slowly begin to come back to this moment. Feel the places in your body where you are connecting to the earth. Deepen your breath. Stretch your arms up over your head, and say a big yes!

You can follow this guided visual imagery with an automatic writing exercise—beginning with *yes* and the image from the visualization that was most meaningful.

If you are working with one client, you won't need to use as many options for total absorption. You will likely know the person and have some idea of the activities she may have enjoyed. You can cue to her specific images that relate to her life, but leave space for her to find images that you know nothing about and that she may have forgotten.

Before beginning the guided visualization, it is important to guide your client in an experience to find a benevolent being who can indeed say yes to her.

Practice: Accessing Personal Affirmation

In this practice, you will be using pranayama breathing: Yogic Three-Part Breath (see Chapter 4) and two rounds of Stair Step Breath (see Chapter 5) along with imagery to evoke a calm and focused state of mind. From this calm state, you can guide your client to allow a personal intention or positive resolve to naturally arise. I conclude this practice with the universal tone of om. This, along with all other aspects of this practice and this book, are optional. Let your own comfort level dictate what you guide.

It might help to let your client know that the tones are universal, as in ahhh-men and sha-lommm, and that using a sound can help extend his breath, which is calming to the central nervous system. Please refer to Chapter 6 for other ways to introduce sound in the treatment room.

If you lead this practice in part or in its entirety, check in with your client afterward. Find out what his intention is. You may need to help him reframe it from "May I . . . " or "I wish . . . " to something more positive and in the present tense, like, "I am . . . " or "_____ breathes through me now." Once this affirmation is established, you can repeat it back to him, using his name. You can also weave it in throughout the session and suggest that your client use it in meditation or yoga practice, or while taking a walk, or even in challenging moments, when he's about to have another beer, or raid the carbohydrate cabinet, or is feeling lonely.

You can guide this experience with your client sitting in a chair or lying in a supine position on the floor.

ACCESSING PERSONAL AFFIRMATION: SCRIPT

We'll be using the breath to clear a pathway through the fog of whatever is blocking you from knowing who you truly are beneath the present mood.

Let's begin with hands on the lower belly. Breathe in through the nostrils so you feel your belly expanding beneath your hands. Exhale and draw the navel back toward the spine. Inhale, 2, 3, 4. Exhale, 2, 3, 4. Beautiful. Now bring your right hand to your ribcage. **Inhale** and feel the breath expanding your belly and then moving into your chest. Exhale, 2, 3, 4. Now bring your right hand to your collarbones. **Inhale** and bring the breath all the way from the belly up to your heart and up under the collarbones. Exhale, 2, 3, 4. This is Yogic Three-Part Breath, Dirga Pranayama.

Now if it's comfortable for you, at the top of your next inhalation, add a short four-count breath retention. **Inhale**, 2, 3, 4. Hold the breath, 2, 3, 4. Exhale, 2, 3, 4. Continue this breath, bringing into your heart's mind an image of a time or a place where you felt peaceful and serene or where you could imagine feeling calm. Find a soothing image, perhaps in nature. If an image doesn't readily arise, simply think the word peace.

Inhale, 2, 3, 4. Hold the breath and see your soothing image, or think the word peace. I am that. Exhale, 2, 3, 4.

Inhale, 2, 3, 4. Hold the breath—see your soothing image. Join me on the exhale with the mantra "so ham," which means I am that. So ham. Beautiful. One more time on your own.

Beautiful. Now, we'll begin the Stair Step Breath. Inhale with little sips of breath through your nostrils, as though you are climbing a mountain. Breathe all the way to the top of the mountain and hold the breath. Look out and see something beautiful. Something that lights you up inside. I am that.

Exhale and slide the breath out.

Again, take little sips, climbing to the top of the mountain. Hold the breath and see something that nourishes your spirit. Or think the word peace. Exhale and gently slide down the mountain.

Allow your own natural breath to find you again. Become aware of breath streaming through your whole body, radiant and pulsing. Find your deep, Yogic Three-Part Breath again, inhaling to the bottom, then the middle and all the way up to the top of your lungs. Then pour the breath out. You may add a light ujjayi ocean sound, by gently constricting the back of the throat and letting the breath ride across the glottis. Waves of breath, lapping against the shores of your body. Ride the waves of your breath home to who you are inside. Home to the ground of your being, beneath the current mood. Beneath the masks you wear in daily life. Home to where you are intimately internally connected. And from this limitless source of your wholeness, invite a heartfelt prayer or a positive resolve to reveal itself to your heart's mind. Place it in the present tense— for example, "I am calm and focused" or "Joy breathes through me now." And breathe it into your heart, polishing your heart. Exhale and release, grounding. Inhale and let your heart shine with the flame of your intention. Exhale and ground here.

With love and acceptance for where you are, no judgment about it, let's create fertile ground for the flowering of your resolve, sacred ground for our session together with the universal healing tone of om. Ommmm.

After leading the experience, ask your client to share his intention with you. It may need a little fine tuning to make it positive and present. You may wish to invite him to say it out loud three times and then repeat it back to him as described above. His intention, known in Sanskrit as a sankalpa, can be a touchstone for the two of you in the session. It may become a therapeutic goal, and it may serve your client in the work he does outside your time together, as part of his meditation practice or simply his positive self-talk.

CHAPTER 9

RELAX: YOGA NIDRA & IREST

"Deep inside you is a fountain of bliss, a fountain of joy. Deep inside your center core is truth, light, love, there is no guilt there, there is no fear there. Psychologists have never looked deep enough."

SRI SRI RAVI SHANKAR

Yoga nidra is a yoga-based meditation technique that can be practiced lying down or sitting up. This ancient yoga meditation can help clients (and therapists) through difficult life challenges, moods, and mental states. The practices of yoga nidra and iRest, the latter developed by psychologist Richard Miller based on the ancient practice of the former, are designed to offer practitioners access to a greater sense of self-awareness, where the opposites of sensation, mood, and belief can be tolerated. The iRest yoga nidra protocol has been shown to be effective in the treatment of PTSD but has much wider applications, including peace of mind for both client and therapist. Yoga nidra practice is easy for beginners and differs from other forms of meditation, in that:

1. It is fully guided.
2. It is usually practiced lying down.
3. It invites the practitioner to consciously bring to mind the

opposites of emotion and belief, including distressing emotion and self-limiting belief.

4. It invites the practitioner into a state of awareness in which these opposites can be embraced with equanimity.

5. It is appropriate for someone suffering from major depression or in recovery from trauma, whereas some other forms of meditation are contraindicated during the acute stages of these conditions.

Mickie Diamond, a clinical social worker in Pittsburgh, was with a client, Katie, who was crying uncontrollably in the emergency room at a psychiatric hospital. Katie's mind was racing with negative thoughts, and she was afraid she would hurt herself. The nurse walked by to tell her that her pulse rate was 135 and that she should calm down. One wonders how the client might have been able to do that if Mickie, who is also a yoga teacher, hadn't been present. Mickie asked the staff to turn off the TV and invited Katie to lie on the couch in the reception area and then led her through a 15-minute yoga nidra experience. "It was wonderful to see her face and body begin to relax. After we finished the exercise, she sat up and told me how calm she felt. The practice helped her get through the night and taught her that her body had the ability to calm itself through natural means."

It can also be a tool for greater self-awareness, as psychologist Deborah Lubetkin suggests. "I am finding yoga nidra to be very helpful when people have left the highly symptomatic phase of their work and are moving into an exploration and integration of who they are now. I think it also helps people to reach their truest potential."

Before giving them a CD to practice with at home, she educates her patients about some of the as-yet unpublished, ongoing trauma research using yoga nidra and iRest with soldiers with PTSD and depression returning from conflict (which can be found online at http://www.irest.us/programs/irest-research-and-programs), as well as many published studies on relaxation and its effect on mood in general (Rani et al., 2011; Manocha, Black, Sarris, & Stough, 2011). She explains how it helps to shift stuck patterns or symptoms. "So far," she says, "I believe it to be most helpful in shifting and integrating broader issues of the self. I don't mean just habits or acute symptoms, but more long-standing parts of people's personality."

After practicing yoga nidra, patients report subtle shifts in perspective. One patient noticed increased clarity in how she communicated with her husband. "She was clear and unwavering," says Lubetkin, "and found herself being very decisive about issues with him and expectations for him. She had no anxiety while doing this. Previously, old emotional patterns including both anxiety and depression would have interrupted this process."

Unlike a guided relaxation, when we practice yoga nidra, we are not trying to relax. In fact, the word *relax* is rarely used. But relaxation happens because we are attending and present to sensation in the body and the breath. Although yoga nidra shares a body scan with most relaxation techniques, including the one taught in the Mindfulness-Based Stress Reduction program, the goals are somewhat different.

Yoga nidra is a form of meditative self-inquiry that, while relaxing the body, opens the mind to greater discernment and self-awareness, and the heart to love and acceptance of what is. It is a powerful tool for clearing away our limiting beliefs and emotions and for living from a more balanced state of mind. The regular practice of yoga nidra can help your clients tolerate aspects of their lives that may seem unpleasant. In the most natural of ways, it teaches practitioners to become less reactive to life's changes and challenges. As such, it can be a tool that helps them self-regulate when events trigger negative cognitions or mood states. Practiced regularly, it can be a pathway to awakening.

Traditional yoga nidra protocols, like those taught by the Bihar School (Swami Satyananda Saraswati) and the Himalayan Institute

(Swami Rama), often move rapidly and mechanically through the body, suggesting that the practitioner visualize or sense each body part. This can be an effective means for stilling the busy mind and aligning it with body sensation and breath. Traditionally, images are provided in the visualization portion that often follows a body scan and breath awareness. Sometimes these images ("a small clean hut," for example) are drawn from the Indian continent and may not be common to clients in the West (Saraswati, 1998).

Richard Miller has adapted this ancient yoga meditation practice in a protocol suitable for Western practitioners that he calls Integrated Restoration or iRest. He has developed protocols that serve specific populations such as those suffering from PTSD or other psychological and physiological imbalances, children, and the homeless. In the iRest protocol, images are not dictated to the practitioner. Instead, they are more likely to be cued, for example, "a place in nature," allowing the client to find an image that suites the current state of mind (Miller, 2005).

The traditional protocols, as well as iRest, progressively release tension accumulated in the muscular, emotional, and mental systems. Muscular tensions "are easily removed by the deep physical relaxation attained in the state of yoga nidra," says Swami Satyananda Saraswati. He goes on to explain how emotional tensions, "which stem from the various dualities," are more difficult to erase and cannot be released through ordinary sleep or relaxation. "Yoga nidra can tranquilize [calm] the entire emotional structure of the mind." Mental tensions, which are the result of excessive mental activity, can be harmonized in yoga nidra practice. "Yoga nidra is the science of relaxation which enables each of us to dive deep down into the realms of the subconscious mind, thereby releasing and relaxing mental tensions, and establishing harmony in all facets of our being" (Saraswati, 1998, p. 23).

Through the practice of yoga nidra, the goal is not only to relax but to transform the personality structure. The studies that have shown an increase in BDNF (brain-derived neurotrophic factor) with the practice of yoga that includes yoga nidra validate this profound change (Gatt et al., 2008). BDNF is a neurotrophin that promotes the neuroplasticity of the brain, allowing us to release old patterns and ingrained habits, changing in profound ways. In yogic terms, we are releasing the *samskaras*, those karmic knots formed in reaction to our actions that create a web of responses that the yogis call the *vasana*. Doesn't this yogic view sound like an astute pretechnological understanding of our neuronal pathways? But it's not just the brain that is affected. Our actions or karma, which are born out of ignorance, leave a residue in the emotional body and the physical body as well. We've all experienced tightness— headaches, muscle tension, stomachache—as the result of a feeling we've blocked. Something happens in our lives and we aren't ready or able to process it, to let the emotion move through. Both hatha yoga practitioners and somatic psychologists believe that what we've experienced is stored in the body. Even when memory is repressed, the body remembers. The stored impressions from past actions can prevent us from experiencing life without preconceived limits. They set up a pattern of response to life, and that is the vasana.

When a samskara is triggered by a thought or a feeling in reaction to something we face, we are likely to respond in a predetermined way. The blueprint for how we are able to love or to not love, even whom we love, is formed through our experiences in our earliest attachments. Our neuronal pathways are set in childhood based on the relationships we have with our parents, and those pathways pave the way for a conditioned response throughout our lives. For example, one of my students grew up with a mother who raged, and though he longs for a relationship without conflict, he keeps getting involved with women who have a violent temper.

Another student, Sheila, grew up living above a nightclub on a river where illegal activities took place. Sheila's father, the charismatic owner of the nightclub, had close ties to organized crime.

No matter what she tells herself she wants in a relationship, if she goes to a party, you can bet that Sheila will hook up with the "bad boy" in the room. Sheila is operating from the web of samskara, her vasana, and has been unable to break the destructive pattern of her relationships.

This web is the template for our conditioned responses to the world, and when we react from our conditioned responses, we are not free. Whether you call it the vasana or use contemporary scientific terms, this template is like a blueprint for our future actions. This template is why certain events or interactions can trigger us into a reaction that may have been set in motion when we were 4 years old. But recent findings in neuroscience have shown that our brains, our neuronal pathways, and even our genes are malleable. Corrective experiences like a good therapeutic relationship can help form new pathways throughout our lives.

When we find ourselves constricting in old patterns of anger or grief, the practice of yoga nidra can immediately dissolve the constriction and progressively change our established mental patterns. When strong emotion does arise, we may begin to witness and welcome it, inquiring into its antecedents, without the need to react. The Dalai Lama says that anger is blind energy. Yoga nidra removes the blindness, so that we can observe the energy without reacting.

Here is Richard Miller's description of why we might choose to engage in a regular iRest yoga nidra practice: "To induce deep relaxation throughout the body and mind, eliminate stress, overcome insomnia, solve personal and interpersonal problems, resolve trauma, and to neutralize and overcome anxiety, fear, anger and depression" (Miller, 2007, p. 1). Once muscular, mental, and emotional tensions begin to dissolve, we are drawn to continue the regular practice of yoga nidra, because the protocol "provides us with guidelines for investigating and going beyond self-limiting beliefs and conditions in order to break free of restrictive patterns so that we can live a contented life, free of conflict, anxiety, fear, dissatisfaction and suffering" (p.171).

BASIC YOGA NIDRA PRACTICE

Let's look at the steps and stages of yoga nidra practice that can
provide benefits beyond those experienced during a guided relaxation in the supine position of Corpse Pose (Savasana) at the end
of yoga class. The following are adapted from Richard Miller's basic
iRest protocol.

BEGINNING STEPS
1. Intention
2. Heartfelt prayer (sankalpa)
3. Inner resource (essential when working with trauma and negative mood states)

ACTUAL PRACTICE
1. Awareness of sensation (*annamaya* kosha)
2. Awareness of breath and energy (*pranamaya* kosha)
3. Awareness of feelings and emotions (*manomaya* kosha)
4. Awareness of thoughts, images, and beliefs (*vijnanamaya* kosha)
5. Awareness of joy, bliss, and love (*anandamaya* kosha)

CONCLUDING STEPS
1. Return to heartfelt prayer
2. Return to awareness of breath
3. Return to awareness of sensation

Woven throughout each of the stages and the last three steps of
returning to ordinary consciousness is awareness of awareness itself.
In leading the practice, this can be expressed as an awareness of
space around the body, a sense of no separation between the energy
that surrounds and the energy that permeates the body, a global
body feeling of energy that expands far beyond the body, a sense
of timelessness, formlessness, emptiness, and abundance, a feeling of
wholeness, a feeling of intimate and eternal connection to all that
is, or an awareness of your "true nature."

Figure 9.1. Richard Miller, PhD, leading iRest yoga nidra at Yoga Yoga in Austin, Texas

Here is a way I might use language to express this: "Is there any separation between the ocean of healing energy that surrounds you, and the rivers of healing energy flowing through you now? You are that energy."

Here is a way Richard Miller might express this awareness of spacious consciousness or awareness itself: "Relinquish observing . . . and become observing itself. Then, as you return to activity, know that you are the awareness that underlies all of life, seemingly separate but, in fact, never separate—always whole and undivided" (Miller, 2007, p. 145).

SUGGESTED YOGA NIDRA MAP

While there are many ways to relax the body and mind that produce the state of yoga nidra, here is a map suggested by Richard Miller that is based on inviting attention to the most sensitive areas of the sensory motor cortex and creating a left lateral shift in the brain, useful in addressing depressed mood (Figure 9.1). The following is a general outline of the actual practice, excluding the beginning and concluding steps. The actual language may be far more detailed (see the full yoga nidra script below).

Head beginning with the mouth
Left hand and arm
Right hand and arm
Torso, front and back
Left leg
Right leg
Major body parts
Global body
Space/awareness/witness

LIFEFORCE YOGA NIDRA SCRIPT

This script follows a kosha model and is inspired by my studies with Richard Miller, PhD. It is an edited version of one of the three yoga nidra experiences I lead on the CD, *LifeForce Yoga Nidra to Manage Your Mood* (see Chapter 11). The practice takes approximately 25 minutes (Figure 9.2).

INTRODUCTION

Let's prepare for yoga nidra.

Come into a supine position, lying on your back with your legs a comfortable distance apart, your palms facing up, and your chin slightly tucked. You may wish to use a cushion or blanket under your knees, an eye pillow to cover your eyes, and a light cover for your body, as your body temperature will lower as you relax. A folded blanket under your head will tilt the chin forward slightly, supporting the mind to relax.

INTENTION

During the practice of yoga nidra, the body may subside for moments into sleep, or into a spacious awareness without thought. Allow my voice to be an anchor, drawing you back into awareness of the present. Let my

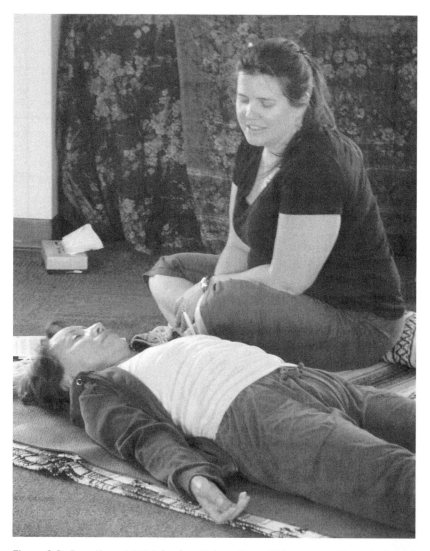

Figure 9.2. Rose Kress, LFYP-2, leading Barbara Rowe, PhD, in yoga nidra at the level 2 LifeForce Yoga Practitioner Training in Tucson, Arizona

words become your words. There's no way to do this wrong. Simply set an intention to remain alert and awake and then let whatever arises be exactly right.

HEARTFELT PRAYER (Sankalpa)

Now join with your own natural rhythm of breath, perhaps using Yogic Three-Part Breath, if you know it, or by simply breathing down into the bottom of the lungs so the belly expands. Ride the waves of your breath home to who you are inside, beneath the current mood, or the costumes you put on. Come home to the ground of your being where you are intimately and eternally connected, that knows no separation. And from this place of wholeness, invite a heartfelt prayer to arise, revealing itself in your heart's mind. What's the burning bush in your heart? The seeds are already present in your life. When you've identified the seed of the longing, plant it in your heart, and say it to yourself in the present tense, as though it's already blossoming. For example, "Peace breathes through me now," or "radiant health breathes through me now," or "I am open and available to give and receive love." This is your deepest intention, your sankalpa. Take two more slow, deep breaths, breathing your sankalpa through every cell. The beginning and end of the yoga nidra practice are the most fertile times for nourishing the seed of your sankalpa. If you plant the sankalpa every day during yoga nidra, that seed will blossom more fully in your life.

INNER RESOURCE
Cultivating inner resources is important when working with trauma and negative mood states.

Imagine now a place where you can be totally relaxed and at ease. Find a soothing image, maybe from nature, maybe in a warm room, or in the arms of a beloved. This is your inner sanctuary, a place you can return to at any time throughout your practice of yoga nidra. It can remain on the altar of your heart so that you can draw upon this soothing image anytime you want a moment of respite in your daily life. Take one more breath with the image of your inner sanctuary in your heart.

AWARENESS OF SENSATION (Annamaya Kosha) WITH GLIMMERS OF PURE AWARENESS (Anandamaya Kosha)
The whole body is lying on the floor. Become aware of the whole body, lying on the floor. A global awareness of sensation radiating through and around the whole body lying on the floor.

Sense each body part as we move systematically, almost mechanically, through the body, beginning with the mouth. Sense deeply into the mouth. Notice sensations at the roof of the mouth, the floor of the mouth. Notice the tongue. Let the tongue fall away from the roof of the mouth. Inner left cheek; inner right cheek. Sense the lips, sensation behind the lips. Whole mouth, hollow and empty. Feel the hollow spaciousness of the mouth as radiant, expansive sensation. All the structures of the mouth, hollow and empty.

Trace a line of sensation flowing from inside the mouth through the hollow tubes of the inner ear canals, all the way out to the hills and valleys of the outer ears. Left ear, right ear, hollow and empty.

Sense the nose, experiencing the hollow spaciousness inside each nostril. Left nostril, right nostril, hollow and empty.

Sense the eyes, those orbs of radiant sensation. Sensation in the eyes flowing all the way back into the structures around the eyes. Cheekbones, left and right. Temples, left and right. Eyebrows, left and right. Bridge of the nose. Sensation between the lids. Upper. Lower. Sensation between the eye lashes. Left eye, right eye, still behind their lids.

Sense the cranium, the whole cranium. Trace a line from the middle of the brow point over the forehead to the crown and all the way back to the back of the head. Notice the neck and the hollow space behind the neck. Sense into the throat—hollow and empty. Sense the hollow notch at the base of the throat.

Breathe into the left side of the body, the whole left side of the body lying on the floor. Follow the sensation in the left shoulder all the way down the arm to the empty spaciousness at the palm of the hand and all the little bones in the fingers. Left thumb, first finger, second finger, third finger, fourth finger. All of the fingers together. Left wrist, elbow, and the hollow space of the armpit. Whole left arm lying on the floor. Feel the whole left arm lying on the floor.

The hollow notch at the base of the throat.

Notice left ribcage, torso, hip, thigh, kneecap, the hollow space behind the kneecap, shin, ankle, all the way down to the hollow space at the sole of the foot and all the little bones in the toes. Big toe, second toe, third toe, fourth toe, fifth toe. All of the toes together. Sensation flowing through the whole left side of the body. Whole left side of the body, radiant, spacious, hollow and empty. Feel the whole left side of the body lying on the floor. Sense into the energy field radiant and shimmering, around the left side of the body lying on the floor.

Sense the hollow notch at the base of the throat.

AWARENESS OF BREATH (Pranamaya Kosha)

Inhale through the sole of the left foot all the way up to the right hemisphere of the brain. Exhale down through the right side. Prana flowing. A circle of breath. Breathing up through the left side and down through the right. Do this two more times on your own.

Breathe your way over to the right side of the body. Sense the right side of the body, lying on the floor. Waves of breath lapping against the right shore of the body. Whole right side of the body lying on the floor.

AWARENESS OF SENSATION, RIGHT SIDE

Sensation in the right shoulder, all the way down the arm to the hollow spaciousness at the palm and all the little bones in the fingers. Right thumb, first finger, second finger, third finger, fourth finger. All of the fingers together. Back of the hand. Right wrist, elbow, and the hollow space of the arm pit. Whole right arm on the mat. Feel the whole right arm on the mat, radiant with sensation.

The hollow notch at the base of the throat.

Notice sensation in the right ribcage, torso, hip, thigh, kneecap, and the hollow space behind the knee, shin, ankle, all the way down to the hollow space at the sole of the foot and all the little bones in the toes. Big toe, second toe, third toe, fourth toe, fifth toe. All the toes together. Sensation flowing through the whole right side of the body. Whole right side of the body, radiant, spacious, hollow and empty. Feel the whole right side of the body lying on the floor. The energy field radiant, shimmering around the right side of the body lying on the floor.

The hollow notch at the base of the throat.

Breathe into both sides of the body simultaneously. Become aware of both sides of the body. Awareness of the whole body lying on the floor. Whole body is lying on the floor.

AWARENESS OF FEELINGS & EMOTIONS (Manomaya Kosha)

Back of the body heavy, sinking into the earth like a stone in sand. Legs, heavy and sinking. Spine, back of the head, arms, heavy and sinking.

From this earthbound density, a lightness begins to arise. Body light and floating. Front of the body, light and shining. Breath flowing through the front of the body—face, chest, abdomen, pelvis, tops of the legs. Front of the body light and floating, whole body light, floating above the floor. Body light and floating like a cloud.

Feel the heaviness in the body and the lightness in the body simultaneously. Body heavy and light. The hollow notch at the base of the throat. The whole body lying on the floor. The whole body lying on the floor and the energy field radiating around the body.

Notice an area of discomfort in your body. Perhaps an unpleasant tightness or numbness. Allow the breath to join the area of discomfort without trying to change anything. Aware of discomfort in the body. Is there an emotion associated with this discomfort? Notice if there's an emotion, perhaps unpleasant, associated with this area of discomfort in the body. No effort. No need to search for words. Simply a felt sense of an emotion woven into the uncomfortable area in the body. Stay present and sense back into the discomfort in the body. Breathe into the area of discomfort.

Is there an area of comfort in the body? Perhaps a pleasant sensation of tingling or wakefulness. Let the breath join with the comfort in the body, without trying to change anything. Simply notice comfort in the body. Is there an emotion associated with this area of comfort? No strain. A word may be there or not. Notice if there's a felt sense of emotion associated with comfort in the body. Stay present and aware of the area of comfort in the body. Breathe into the area of comfort.

Go back and forth between the area of discomfort in the body and the area of comfort in the body. Take two long breaths into the area of discomfort and feel the emotion, if there is one, associated with that discomfort.

Take two long breaths into the area of comfort, and feel the emotion, if there is one, associated with the pleasant feeling in the body.

AWARENESS OF THOUGHTS, IMAGES, & BELIEFS (Vijnanamaya Kosha)
This section is included in the longer versions on the iRest CDs and on the LifeForce Yoga Nidra CD.

AWARENESS OF JOY, BLISS, & LOVE (Anandamaya Kosha)
Sensing back now into a greater timeless awareness, expanded and spacious, aware of both discomfort in the body and comfort in the body. Embracing both the discomfort and the unpleasant emotion, and also the comfort in the body and the pleasant emotion. Can you sense back into a spacious awareness where discomfort and comfort, pleasant and unpleasant, heaviness and lightness can live in the body-mind? Awareness expanding, formless and timeless. Awareness aware of itself.

Awareness of the energy around the body, bliss expanding and spacious like a great cosmic smile. Invite the smile to enter your heart. Maybe a memory comes—a moment of happiness. Inhale and breathe the moment around your heart. Heart smiling. Your eyes. Eyes smiling. Your cheeks. Cheeks smiling. Memory dissolves. Whole body smiling. Blissful smile extending beyond the limits of your physical body lying on the floor. Bliss expanding beyond the limits of this room. Bliss spacious and expanding beyond the limits of this country. Bliss spacious, radiant, expanding beyond the limits of this planet. Bliss shimmering eternally, intimately.

No separation between the ocean of healing energy that surrounds you and the rivers of healing energy flowing through you now.

From this expanded place of spacious awareness, everything you need is flowing though you now. Whole. Here. Now. No separation.

RETURNING TO HEARTFELT PRAYER (Sankalpa), AWARENESS OF
BREATH, AWARENESS OF SENSATION

Begin to notice your body lying on the floor. Notice the sounds in the room. Deepening your breath, breathing into your wholeness, breathe your sankalpa through you now. It's already present. Nourish the seed with your breath and your attention. As you breathe your heartfelt intention through you, completing your yoga nidra practice, you are fertilizing the seed of intention that will manifest fully, blossoming in every facet of your life.

As you end your yoga nidra practice and return to your daily life, resolve to stop throughout your day. Pause for a moment in the middle of your activity, in conversation, at mealtime, or at your desk. Simply pause and sense back into this greater awareness that you are. Not separate. Whole. Thank you for practicing yoga nidra today.

YOGA NIDRA & TRAUMA

Yoga nidra can be useful for a person who has suffered trauma or for whom depression or overpowering emotion is present, as the guidance helps the practitioner begin to disidentify with the trauma or negative mind state. This might be expressed in the following ways: "Pure awareness has never been traumatized." "My body may have been traumatized, but my true nature has never been touched or tainted" (Miller, 2007).

To avoid repeating old patterns of dissociation, it's important that the client or student (especially one who has been traumatized) be fully grounded in the sensations in the body and the breath. Once it's safe to be living from the neck down again, then guidance may be given to step back into awareness itself. It is important to practice the grounding stages of body sensation and breath regularly until the practitioner feels that it's safe to feel sensation and to fully breathe into the body. Once there is a thorough reclaiming of all that has been split off and dissociated from in the physical, emotional, and mental bodies, then, when you feel the client is ready, your guidance can include an exploration of the opposites and the expansion into awareness.

Robin Carnes is a yoga therapist and iRest teacher who works with soldiers at Walter Reed Army Hospital. The work is extremely gratifying, she says. After his first yoga nidra experience, one service member came up to her and quietly said, "I feel like I've been waiting my whole life to come here." The soldiers at Walter Reed often suffer from high levels of physical pain due to their injuries, in addition to multiple diagnoses of sleep apnea, PTSD, and depression. One soldier confided in her that he had been in terrible pain for so long he could not remember how it felt not to be in pain. After his 10th yoga nidra session, he told Robin that his legs, arms, and back felt numb. Robin asked him if it felt unpleasant. He said, "No, it feels fantastic! I am not in pain!" The next day he told her that after he left the session, he felt so much energy that he could have run around the building 10 times, and he'd gone until 3:00 A.M. (11 hours) without taking anything for pain. "He was ecstatic," says Robin.

When working with clients with a history of trauma, it's important to help them establish an inner resource before you begin. Sometimes memories or emotions are triggered that create discomfort. If a client knows that she has permission to stop attending to your words and take time to self-soothe with a pleasant memory or a safe place, she has control over her experience, which increases her feeling of self-efficacy, and she is less likely to be flooded by negative emotion. Clients may begin to use their inner resource in their daily lives. One soldier told Robin that a lot of feelings and images had come up in his group therapy session earlier in the day that left him feeling overwhelmed. When he put his attention on his inner resource and pictured himself running along the river, having a wonderful time with his son, it calmed him down. He told her he'd used the image many times at home between sessions with her.

CHAPTER 10

WELCOMING IT ALL: YOGIC SELF-INQUIRY (Svadhyaya)

Those ancient yogis were astonishingly perceptive about human psychology. They supported the idea of self-inquiry, known as *svadhyaya*, which literally means self-study. They understood that working with the opposites of mood and belief can help us find the middle ground. "When negative cognitions arise," said Patanjali, the 200 C.E. codifier of the *Yoga Sutras*, "cultivate their opposites" (Hartranft, 2003, II, 33). Patanjali's *Yoga Sutras* is a collection of 196 aphorisms on the nature of consciousness and awakening. The *Yoga Sutras* is a foundational text referred to by most modern yoga schools. The aphorisms were likely passed orally from master to student, until they were written down around 200 C.E. In their insight, they share concepts and language with Mahayana Buddhism.

EXPLORING THE OPPOSITES

Working with polarities in a process of self-inquiry that includes the body is common to many modalities of psychotherapy today, including cognitive-behavioral therapy, internal family systems therapy, eye movement desensitization and reprocessing (EMDR), and, in particular, coherence therapy. As psychotherapist Bonnie Badenoch points out in *The Brain-Savvy Therapist's Workbook*, when there are negative beliefs or implicit memories rooted in trauma, "we can't dig them out with left-mode [left-hemisphere] pressure

. . . but we can invite them into experience by opening our attention to body sensations, behavioral impulses and feelings" (2011, p. 188). Badenoch provides strong evidence that the memories stored incoherently in what she calls right-mode (or right-hemisphere) processing need a treatment approach that uses "right-mode language that embodies the visceral experience." She goes on to say, "Whether or not words are involved, the firing patterns that change [neuronal patterns, thus beliefs, behavior, and even memory] involve the right-mode neural nets that hold implicit memory. If this process is mediated by language, it seems to be most effective when the words have some of these qualities: poetic, direct, concrete, metaphorical, fresh, or descriptive" (p. 189).

The language of yoga "embodies the visceral experience" and is often poetic and metaphorical in its attempt to describe the indescribable experience of union, the embracing of the opposites.

Clients who have suffered repeated forms of abuse, especially early in life, have often found some self-protection and solace in dissociation. In fact, Roger Woolger, Jungian psychologist and author of *Other Lives, Other Selves*, depathologizes dissociative states. He talks about the "Persephone Woman," whom he believes has easier access to psychic states or other realms because she has cultivated that ability to disconnect from apparent reality in her will to protect herself (Woolger, 1988). However, although the Persephone Woman who experienced chronic, repetitive incidents of abuse may have an explicit memory of the events—left-mode processing at work—because she dissociated during the trauma, that memory may be completely devoid of emotional content. On the other hand, people who experience shock trauma—caused by war or other catastrophic events—who are then diagnosed with PTSD may have no coherent memory of the event. In the fight-or-flight response, increased cortisol has flooded the limbic brain, preventing the hippocampus from doing its job of storing memories in chronological order. Rather, the memories are implicit. They are incoherent and fraught with emotion.

In both cases, "we need," says Daniel Siegel, author of *Mindsight* and *The Mindful Therapist*, "therapeutic strategies that address both sides of the brain, that invite emotional content (right side of the brain/implicit memory) back into explicit memory and logical narrative (left side/explicit memory) back into emotional coherence" (quoted in Wylie, 2004b, p. 47). This is what yoga does in general, by activating the parasympathetic nervous system and creating greater heart rate variability, an indicator that we can flow more easily from appropriately aroused states to appropriately calm states. But in particular, the yoga-based self-inquiry strategies that include yoga nidra, discussed in Chapter 9, work with the opposites by beginning with body and breath and imagery, which, as we've seen in Chapter 8, circumvents the linear narrative of left-mode processing and goes directly to what has been exiled, be it memory or emotion.

In both yoga nidra and in the yoga-based self-inquiry intervention discussed in this chapter, we guide the client to experience the polarities of sensation, belief, and emotion, first alternately, and then simultaneously. The originators of coherence therapy, Bruce Ecker and Laurel Hulley, call this process the "juxtaposition experience," described as a "richly experiential, special form of affectively anchored cognitive dissonance" (Badenoch, 2011; Ecker, 2010). In the yoga-based tradition, we then invite the client through the right-mode processing strategies (meditation, breath awareness, sensory awareness, imagery) into a more spacious, global awareness that can embrace the opposites.

SVADHYAYA: EMOTIONAL CLEARING THROUGH SELF-INQUIRY

Underlying all the yoga skills and interventions in this book, including self-inquiry, is a philosophy of yoga that, when understood, can itself be a source of transformation. Yoga tells us that we are deeply and intimately connected, and it is our ignorance (*avidya*) that veils us from this truth. All the yoga tools we use are ultimately designed to clear the space, dispelling this ignorance of our true nature, and thus put us back in touch with our wholeness, beneath mood and symptoms and even our attachments to what we love. We clear the space with the many skills I've outlined in this book, but it helps to have a roadmap. It helps to know that our ultimate destination is to return home to ourselves, that which is unsullied by the tribulations and traumas of our apparent reality. Yoga teaches us that we are born whole. Little by little we begin to separate through the losses and betrayals of growing up in an imperfect world. If our earliest attachments were less than secure, or if the parenting we received was invasive or distant, we may have had to separate in ways that walled us off from the knowledge of that wholeness. Some of us have carried that separation throughout our lives in the form of depression or other mood disorders. Yoga gives us a visceral sense of our wholeness when we practice the many tools we've covered so far. But it's also more than practice. In the popular imagination, yoga is about movement and perhaps breathing exercises and meditation, so I've met that expectation in this book by beginning with the practices. Now that you're still with me, we can conclude with a more philosophical approach. However, this chapter could just as easily have begun the book. The principle of self-study (svadhyaya) is one of the most essential elements that constitute yoga's power to heal, and it may have nothing to do with a yoga mat or a meditation cushion. This power to heal is rooted in an understanding of the philosophy of yoga, and for that, we can turn again to Patanjali.

In Chapter 1, I referred to Patanjali's prescription for addressing our suffering: "Tapas svadhyaya Ishvara-pranidhana kriya yoga," which in Chip Hartranft's elegant translation means, "Yogic action has three components—discipline, self-study, and orientation toward the ideal of pure awareness" (2003, p. 21). This is the core instruction for the yogic view of change, for how we can achieve "union in action" (kriya yoga) that arises from the clarity of true self-awareness.

In contemporary life, we tend to think of self-study as therapy—whether it's developing the witness on our meditation cushions through mindfulness practice, or on our yoga mats as we observe body sensations, thoughts, and feelings without reaction, or borrowing the witness consciousness of the therapist. The yogis have offered us a number of self-inquiry exercises using self-study to cultivate greater self-awareness. They are well suited to the consultation room, and we will explore one of them in this chapter.

We know how easy it is to numb out, to find ways to distract ourselves from our own difficult emotions. When painful feelings arise for clients, unhealthy patterns may reassert themselves—default strategies like bingeing on food, drugs, or alcohol, zoning out on television, or oversleeping. Sometimes even healthy strategies help us and our clients avoid being honest with ourselves. We can become compulsive about exercise. Even yoga practice can be an escape from what's right in front of us—a pressing thought or emotion that needs our attention. Yoga asanas can be practiced mindlessly, obsessively, in a driven way that blocks true self-inquiry. And meditation, too, can be an escape from difficult emotions and thoughts.

But when yoga is practiced with attention to breath and sensation, emotions arise on their own, daring us to take a look. If we don't, the body constricts. We experience stomach discomfort or a headache. When we don't turn away from what is arising, we have the perfect opportunity to cultivate self-study (svadhyaya). Exploring the opposites of belief and emotion through the doorway of the body softens our reactivity to life. Instead of constricting around a hurtful memory or clinging to a happier one, we can move back and forth, ultimately standing in the place of awareness—both are necessary; both are the essence of life in a human body. This timeless teaching from the yoga tradition is being validated by current research on the "reconsolidation window." Neuroscientists at New York University have shown that spending at least 10 minutes with the negative belief or feeling before moving to its opposite may help release the grip of the negative thought form, including fear (Schiller et al., 2010). The experience of the practitioners who use nondual interventions that explore and welcome the opposites in unity like the one in this chapter and the iRest protocol in Chapter 9 is that staying on the negative side of the polarity for 10 minutes can be overwhelming to some people. In general, more than 2 to 3 minutes is excessive. Rather than holding the negative for 10 minutes, we take the client back and forth between positive and negative, holding the focus on each between 1 and 3 minutes.

What follows is a step-by-step protocol for one yoga-based self-inquiry intervention, culled from the nondual tradition of Kashmiri Shaivism, as taught by Jean Klein and his student, Richard Miller. The intervention below is based on my individual work with Richard Miller, the Integrative Restoration Training (iRest) he offers, and modifications based on my own exploration with students and clients. Throughout this protocol, you are probing for your client's cognitions, without intervening to help or support with your own best intentions. As Miller says, "We never impose upon or try to change people. We never tell people how they 'should' be. Rather, we help them explore their actual first-hand experience of sensation, feeling, and thinking. When there is total freedom to explore and be just as we are, truth, insight, and change manifest spontaneously" (quoted in Weintraub, 2011).

NONDUAL INTERVENTION: BASIC INSTRUCTIONS

1. Invite your client to try this practice when he seems stuck in a limiting concept about himself, or when a lot of emotion rises to the surface during your work together.
2. Use your client's words to mirror back.
3. Keep it simple, concrete, not abstract. Resist the use of words like "core belief," "the opposite of the core belief," "nondual," or "union." These terms can sound too psychological or spiritual.
4. Resist "helping" by supplying ideas, words, or images.

5. If possible, invite your client to lie in a supine position. Use props to ensure comfort.

   a. Dig for the core belief or feeling. Say, "Is there something underneath 'He doesn't respect me'?" (Repeat the client's words.) The client may ultimately say, "I'm unlovable," or "I'm not worthy of respect," or "There's something wrong with me." Keep repeating, "Is there something underneath . . . " until you feel you've reached the core belief or emotion.

   b. Once you feel you have reached the core belief, ask where it resides in the body. For example, "Where is 'I'm not worthy of love' [repeat the client's words] in your body?"

   c. Repeat what is said. For example, "Breathe into that 'I'm not worthy' in your gut."

   d. Does it have a color?

   e. Repeat what is said. It may or may not have a color. For example, "Breathe into that fiery red 'I'm not worthy' in your belly."

   f. Is there an image for the color and belief in the body part?

   g. Repeat what is said. "Breathe into [the belief, the color image] in your [body part]. Allow yourself to feel it fully." For example, "Breathe into that fiery red ball in black chains of unworthiness in your belly. Allow yourself to really feel it fully."

      1. Continue guiding, repeating phrase 9 for several minutes, asking what is being sensed and repeating it back.

      2. Watch breath and facial expression.

   h. Invite the opposite: "If [repeat color and core belief] weren't there in your [body part], what extreme opposite might be there instead? For example, "If that fiery red ball of unworthiness weren't there in your belly, what would be the opposite belief, the most extreme, far-fetched opposite that might be there instead?" We want the client to experience the opposite of the negative polarity for two reasons. First, so he can have a visceral sense of that strong positive belief in his body. Second, if we settle too quickly into a belief like, "I'm good enough the way I am," there's no middle ground. It's not really the opposite of "I'm unworthy."

   i. Repeat back what the client says. For example, he may say, "I am a hero," or "I am adored by everyone I meet." Again, please note: "I am worthy" isn't strong or extreme enough at this point. If something moderate is said, like "I'm worthy," or "I'm okay just the way I am," you may ask if that is the most extreme opposite of the initial belief. Encourage an outrageous opposite. Tell your client that it's okay to pretend or to fantasize.

   j. Ask if he can find the positive polarity in his body. For example, "Where does 'I am a beloved saint' live in your body?"

   k. Repeat what is said. For example, "Breathe into the beloved saint at your brow point."

   l. "Is there a color associated with the beloved saint at your brow point?"

   m. Repeat what is said. For example, "Breathe into the beloved saint, surrounded by bright white light, at your brow point." It may not have a color.

   n. "Is there an image associated with 'I am a beloved saint' surrounded by bright white light at your brow point?" It may not have an image.

   o. "Breathe into [the opposite of core belief, color, image] in your [body part]. Allow yourself to feel it fully." For example, "Breathe into the image of yourself leading a circle dance with everyone you know on top of the mountain, surrounded in white light. Breathe into that 'I am a beloved saint.'"
      1. Continue for several minutes.
      2. Watch for breath, facial expression to change.

   p. Invite your client to move back and forth between the

opposites. For example, "I know this may not feel pleasant, but I'm going to invite you back into that 'I am unworthy of love,' that fiery red ball in chains in your belly. Take a few breaths feeling that 'I am unworthy' again." Take three or four breaths here.

q. Watch for signs of change in breathing and facial expression and then invite the client to breathe back into the positive extreme. For example, "Let's go back to the image of yourself leading a circle dance with everyone you know on top of the mountain, surrounded in white light. Breathe into that 'I am a beloved saint.'" Take three or four breaths here.

r. Invite your client to go back and forth on his own two more times, taking two or three breaths in each place.

s. When you can see that your client is breathing into the positive opposite belief or feeling (breathing calm, face soft, often a smile), invite him to "let a third belief arise—something between the [image/belief] in your [body part] and the [image/opposite belief] in your [body part]." For example, "Can you step back into a spacious awareness of both the 'I am unworthy of love' in your belly and the 'I am a beloved saint' at your brow point and allow a third idea to arise, something between 'I am unworthy' and 'I am a saint'?"

t. From this third place, invite the client to create an affirmation that is rooted in the present. This is usually an "I am" or "I have" statement. For example, "I am worthy and deserving of respect."

   1. Invite the client to repeat it three times, using his name.

   2. Use his name and say it back to him three times. Hearing it repeated can be a very powerful experience for the client, as Francoise Adan describes in Chapter 8.

Application

I would suggest practicing with this formula without introducing other techniques until it's familiar to you. Once you learn it, you may find it adaptable to all kinds of clinical applications. Robin Carnes, the iRest teacher we met in Chapter 9 who works at Walter Reed Hospital, soon to be Walter Reed National Military Medical Center, used it with a soldier when a strong reaction arose during a yoga nidra experience.

Since returning from Iraq, Frederick had suffered from terrible nightmares. He had been working with a social worker to address these dreams in a multidisciplinary treatment program at Walter Reed, developed to treat soldiers with PTSD. Through a set of unusual circumstances, Frederick was the only soldier there for the iRest yoga nidra practice. Robin was especially attentive to him as he went into the practice. It had been her experience that soldiers are far more likely to have an abreaction when they are alone. "I imagine," says Carnes, "that subconsciously they feel free enough to take the lid off. Often more difficult memories and emotions emerge, when the other members of their group are not there to witness."

Halfway through the 45-minute session, Frederick's body stiffened and he opened his eyes. Carnes describes touching his arm and calling his name, during which he continued to look distressed. Frederick told her that he had had a terrifying nightmare. Using the self-inquiry protocol, Carnes asked him gently but repeatedly to tell her about the dream interspersed with questions about his physical experience. "What sensation do you feel in your mouth?" she asked as he described the dream. "What sensation do you feel in your tongue? What sensation do you feel in your palms?" Carnes's cues to attend to physical sensations kept him grounded in the present as he described the dream, and she asked in a way that would evoke a description rather than a yes or no answer. Black Dobermans, covered in blood, were chasing him, growling viciously and baring their teeth. He knew they wanted to kill him.

After describing the dream, his agitation remained high. As frightening images continued to arise, Carnes invited him to find the sensation in his body. For 10 minutes, she repeated his words as he told her about the frozen feeling in his gut and lower back. As she asked him to describe it, the feeling changed from one sensation to another. When he occasionally tried to analyze the dream, Carnes redirected him to a description of body sensation.

After relaying the dream, Frederick said he still felt startled, so Carnes invited him to feel deeply into and then describe the physical sensations of being startled. "My blood is spurting in my veins; my heart is beating fast; my chest feels tight." Carnes repeated every description, using Frederick's words. After each repetition, she waited a moment and then asked him, "What are you aware of now?"

Eventually, Carnes probed for the opposite of the startled feeling. "If feeling startled weren't there, what opposite emotion would be there?" He closed his eyes and sensed into the feeling again, and then his face lit up and he said, "Joy." Carnes repeated "joy" and asked him how that joy would feel in his body. Again he paused to feel into the question. Then he opened his eyes and moved his arms and hands in full gestures. "It feels open and free, open and free," he said. "Feel that," Carnes said. She invited him to remember a time when he'd felt really joyful and open and free. He closed his eyes again, and when he smiled, it was clear to Carnes that this feeling was accessible to him. After a few minutes of supporting the joyful, free, and open feeling, Carnes suggested he sense back into the startled feeling. He tried, but he couldn't find that feeling again. "When he opened his eyes," she says, "his smile was broad and victorious."

Carnes acknowledged to Frederick what he had been able to do, how he had stayed with the process and not shut down or tightened up. "I want to go back in there and deal with those dogs," he said, "so they don't come after me again." Carnes sat quietly with Frederick as he lay with his eyes closed. She could see by his relaxed facial expression that he was calmly creating a different scene with the dogs. "You could tell that a lot was happening in his inner world," she says. After a few minutes, she asked him if he could see the dogs. He told her that the dogs were turned away from him now. "He was smiling with a kind of wonder on his face. I asked if they were bloody like before. He said no, they were all cleaned up and they were walking in front of him. Then his face broke into a much bigger smile, and he said that the dogs were out in front protecting him." Carnes was quiet, letting Frederick stay with the image, before repeating back what he had said. "The dogs are protecting you. The dogs are out in front of you, protecting you." She let him bask in the image for several minutes, now and then, repeating the new image back to him.

When he opened his eyes, they were radiant, Carnes says. She acknowledged him for his great work and asked how he was feeling. He told her that he had an enormous amount of energy and wanted to go running. "This was a guy whose lower back pain was almost completely debilitating a few days earlier," she said.

In this case, Frederick's identification with the trauma was so profound, that Carnes chose to let the session end with the positive reframing of his dream experience. This was certainly enough to help Frederick and to give him solace. Eventually, with continued practice, Frederick might be able to tolerate both the negative and positive dog imagery. The nondual practices provide us with a way to disidentify with one side or the other side of the pairs of opposites. In sharing them with our your clients, you help them cultivate a calmer, less reactive state of mind.

CHAPTER 11

ON THE MAT
& MORE:
REFERRALS,
RESOURCES,
& TRAINING

So far, our focus has been on yoga-based practices that are safely suited to your treatment room. As I made clear in the introduction, none of these practices requires a yoga mat or blocks or a strap. However, after learning a breathing practice or a mudra from you that has helped him self-soothe or muster the energy needed to make changes in his life, your client may likely be interested in trying a yoga class or finding a yoga therapist who can offer him individual sessions. To make a recommendation that is best suited to your client, it's important for you to be aware of the various options.

If the class your client tries at his health club is too difficult or too touchy-feely or if he is the only man in the room, he may be discouraged. If she's a couch potato and can't get up to change the channel when the remote dies, it's unlikely she will respond to a vigorous yoga class that begins with ten Sun Salutations. If she's a type A personality, experiencing high levels of anxiety, she may become even more anxious in a restorative yoga class. I once took my high-strung 20-something niece Jody, who was visiting from New York City, to a friend's yoga class. The teacher started the class in a supine restorative position. We were supposed to relax over a bolster with an eye pillow covering our eyes, while the teacher went around the room waving lavender oil and giving neck massages. Suddenly, over the reclined body of my niece, I heard the teacher exclaim, "I have never seen anyone text in a yoga class before!" Obviously Jody would have been better off starting with those Sun Salutations, burning off a bit of steam, before she could relax.

To avoid the same mistake, it's a good idea to be informed about the various styles of yoga and the teachers in your community. In most areas, you can do a Google search to find local studios and read about the teachers and their individual approach. Don't hesitate to call the teacher and, better yet, take the class yourself, so you know for sure what your clients will receive. It's great to get to know yoga teachers in your community, because they are an excellent referral source. When I was teaching regular daily classes in Tucson, I kept the business cards of those to whom I referred on hand. Sometimes tamped-down emotions surface in class or a student might have a strong emotional release on the mat. After class, I was often asked if I knew a psychotherapist who was open to yoga, and I referred many of my students to those I trusted.

In addition to searching the bios of teachers at local studios, other reliable sources on the Internet list teachers in your area. The primary certifying organization is the Yoga Alliance (www.yogaalliance.org). This organization maintains a registry of yoga teachers who have met minimum teaching standards at the 200-hour level and at the professional 500-hour level. It also registers yoga schools whose teacher training programs maintain those standards.

Another good resource for finding a qualified teacher or yoga therapist in your area is the International Association of Yoga Therapists (IAYT, www.iayt.org). IAYT maintains a database of its members. Currently, each member's profile includes yoga training, credentials, and teaching style. The IAYT also maintains a list of yoga therapy training programs. On this list are full yoga therapy training programs that cover all aspects of well-being—structural issues like lower back pain and joint problems, breathing issues like COPD and asthma, and emotional and mental imbalances as well as spiritual imbalances. These training programs often require years of study.

IAYT's standards committee is currently at work defining the requirements for the designation "yoga therapist." They are considering the whole range of yoga education and experience, so those standards will be quite rigorous, far beyond what is required by the Yoga Alliance to become a yoga teacher. That being said, by the current proposed draft of standards, a yoga therapist as defined by IAYT will have a general knowledge of emotional and mental health issues from a yoga perspective, but will not necessarily have specialty training in that area. Below I have included a list of general yoga therapy programs, as well as specialty programs that focus on mental health issues, including the LifeForce Yoga Practitioner Training I developed for both yoga teachers and psychotherapists, Phoenix Rising Yoga Therapy, and Integrative Restoration (iRest). These specialty trainings in mental health are available to therapists who may not wish to invest the time and study required to become a yoga therapist or yoga teacher, but are still interested in incorporating some elements of yoga practice into their therapy work. This list is by no means exhaustive but includes the well-known programs that will likely meet future IAYT requirements.

Before we consider the more advanced yoga therapy and specialty trainings, let's look at the different styles of yoga so that you can make a referral suited to your client's constitution and needs.

A REVIEW OF YOGA STYLES

Hatha yoga means physical force, so the term, which covers all yoga styles, almost always includes a yoga mat. As we've discussed throughout the book, it's important to match the client's style, mood, and constitution with a practice that she will enjoy and that will move her toward balance. You neither want to exacerbate her extreme tendencies nor bore or overwhelm her with something so alien to her style, mood, and constitution that she tells you after her first class, "I tried yoga, and it's not for me."

What follows is a description of some of the more prominent styles with recommendations about which of your clients might benefit from them.

Iyengar Yoga was the first hatha yoga style to find a welcome reception in the West, and with its emphasis on proper alignment, it is ideal for those with physical injuries. The study of Iyengar Yoga provides a firm foundation in asana practice and has been shown to be effective for those suffering from depression and anxiety (Shapiro, 2007). However, initially and for many years, B. K. S. Iyengar believed that the body must be prepared for the breath. Although he has changed his approach in recent years, students must be deemed ready before pranayama breathing is taught, which for some Iyengar teachers means the student must first be adept in the execution of poses. What this means is that your clients may not learn a number of breathing practices that might enhance the effect of their posture sequence in addressing mood. However, there are several highly regarded Iyengar teachers who do specialize in working with depressed mood, including Patricia Walden, Karin Stephan, and Kofi Busia.

Anusara Yoga, an offshoot of Iyengar Yoga, developed by the master teacher John Friend, does include simple pranayama breathing (Ujjayi or Ocean-Sounding Victory Breath) along with alignment details and an emphasis on opening the heart. This style of yoga may appeal to clients suffering from anxiety or depression who are relatively fit and active.

If your client is fit and under 30, one of the more vigorous yoga styles may be appropriate for both anxiety and depression. Your client may enjoy a beginning class in **Ashtanga**, **Power Yoga**, or another form of **Vinyasa Flow** (**Jivamukti**, **Forrest Yoga**, or **White Lotus**, to name a few of the most popular). These classes will include Ocean-Sounding Victory Breath (Ujjayi) (see Chapter 4) and Sun Salutations, as well as both standing and floor poses.

Athletes are often attracted to **Bikram Yoga**, a series of 26 poses practiced in a heated room. While a brief pranayama breathing practice is led at the beginning and end of this series, there is less emphasis on the breath during the posture practice. Some clients will find the heat intolerable, and others will love the detoxing effect of all that sweat. Be aware that the instruction is scripted and tough, so, other than an occasional correction in a pose, there is little attention to a student's individual needs. Bikram Yoga is light on spirituality, which may be a plus for some clients.

Other schools of yoga that incorporate a standard series of poses, along with more pranayama, meditation, and relaxation than those outlined above, include **Sivananda Yoga**, **Integral Yoga**, and **Kripalu Yoga**. All three are suited to most practitioners, although Kripalu Yoga, which has always maintained three levels of practice (gentle, moderate and vigorous), is adaptable to all body types, ages, and mood states. Kripalu teachers are trained to take a compassionate approach with an emphasis on self-acceptance and spiritual transformation, so the practice is well suited to a client who suffers from depression. Offshoots of Kripalu Yoga include **Prana Yoga**, **Integrative Yoga**, **LifeForce Yoga**, and **Nosara Yoga**.

Those who need a gentle approach may find that starting with a **Restorative** practice that includes props to support the body, or **Yin Yoga**, in which poses are held for several minutes, is appealing. Both styles can also be integrated into a more active practice. In other words, restorative poses and longer holds are a good doorway in for a client with depression, before ramping up the energy during the session. And they can provide a good doorway out for someone who is anxious and may wish to meet the excess energy with a more active practice before calming the energy down.

Viniyoga, as developed by Gary Kraftsow and taught through the American Viniyoga Institute, along with other forms of hatha yoga instructed from the Krishnamacharya* tradition as interpreted through his son, master teacher Desikachar, are designed to be led individually and make it a point to meet the current condition with a practice that includes postures, pranayama breathing, mantra chanting, and meditation.

Kundalini Yoga, as was taught by Yogi Bhajan, emphasizes breath and repetitive movement. A full class of Kundalini Yoga provides an excellent program for someone in a depressed state, but may be too stimulating for someone experiencing high levels of anxiety. While mounting evidence suggests that certain individual practices, known as kriya meditations, can be beneficial when done separately, caution is advised in recommending a general Kundalini class to someone with high levels of anxiety, bipolar disorder with manic tendencies, or more serious forms of mental illness, as some of the practices are contraindicated.

Finally, **LifeForce Yoga**, which may be combined with any of the yoga styles listed above, enhances the mood-balancing effect of the posture sequence by incorporating timeless practices that current research has shown are effective in treating depression and anxiety. For those who have physical limitations that prevent a full yoga posture practice, the yoga strategies taught in the LifeForce Yoga program, including mudra, mantra, pranayama breathing, relaxation, and meditation techniques can be especially effective for managing mood.

In addition to the styles of yoga listed above and the many fine teachers who instruct them, there are other master yoga teachers of note who have studied in one of these traditions but have gone on to develop what they teach from the profound information they receive from the laboratory of their own practice. Such teachers include Rama Jyoti Vernon, Angela Farmer, Victor von Kooten,

---

*Krishnamacharya (November 18, 1888–November 3, 1989) was an Indian hatha yoga adept, one of the first master yogis whose teachings reached the West through his students, B. K. S. Iyengar (Iyengar Yoga), Patabi Jois (Ashtanga Yoga), Desikachar, Indira Devi, and Vanda Scaravelli.

Frank Jude Boccio, and the yogi who introduced many Westerners to yoga through her long-running PBS television program, Lilias Folan.

Even more important than directing your client to the right style of yoga is directing her to a teacher with whom she will feel comfortable. If your client is suffering, the container of self-acceptance the teacher creates for the class is essential.

INTEGRATING YOGA TOOLS INTO YOUR WORK WITH CLIENTS: SUPPORTING PRACTICE MATERIALS

A number of practice DVDs, CDs, and online videos can facilitate your client's at-home practice. One short protocol designed specifically for home use that accompanies psychotherapy and is being used in an ongoing clinical trial is now available on my Web site, www.yogafordepression, as an audio download with an accompanying manual. The entire 30-minute practice includes a centering meditation, simple warm-up movements, and an active meditation that incorporates the energizing version of the LifeForce Yoga Chakra-Clearing Meditation (mudras and mantras designed for depressed mood) described in Chapter 7. However, your client can choose to do the breathing practice and meditation only in less than 15 minutes.

Practice Audio CDs

Below is a list of audio CDs that I created, all of which are available on my Web site, www.yogafordepression.com.

Breathe to Beat the Blues contains an introduction and a sequence of 10 pranayama breathing exercises to help you calm your mind and elevate your mood. The practice begins with a centering meditation and ends with a long relaxation. The breathing exercises alternate between energizing and calming practices, and the liner notes instruct the listener in how to arrange the tracks to address the presenting mood state.

LifeForce Yoga Bhavana: Say Yes to Yourself (Chapter 8) includes breathing exercises, gentle stretching, mantra, a guided relaxation, and a writing exercise, designed to support a positive outlook on the future.

The **LifeForce Yoga Chakra-Clearing Meditation** (Chapter 7) is a technique that combines several strategies to focus and clear the mind. There is empirical evidence that this practice helps those who suffer from anxiety and depression, along with obsessive-compulsive disorder, characterized by intrusive and repetitive thoughts. The technique engages the mind with sound and breath and hand gestures called mudras. Experienced meditators can benefit from these techniques too. If you regularly sit, it helps to have a beginning practice to clear your mind so that more of your 20 or 30 minutes is spent floating on the still pond of your mind, observing the ripples and waves of your thoughts and feelings, and less on drowning in them.

LifeForce Yoga Nidra to Manage Your Mood and Relaxation for Sleep (Chapter 9) includes practices inspired by the psychologist Richard Miller. The longest one is just over 40 minutes, and it deeply relaxes and dissolves long-established emotional and mental patterns in the process of relaxing the body. The 20-minute practice balances mood, relaxes the mind, and gives the body a boost of physical energy. The final practice is shorter and is designed for a restful night's sleep.

The following are audio CDs I recommend.

Chill Children: Guided Relaxation With Global Family Yoga includes seven short visualizations spoken by Mira Binzen. The practices are based on yoga nidra and will guide children and their families into deep states of relaxation.

Deep Relaxation: Guided Yoga Nidra is guided by popular Kripalu Yoga teacher. Jennifer Reis, whose voice is melodic and whose guidance is full of imagery. Track 1 includes a chakra experience. Track 2 is a journey into the Native American Seven Directions with Eagle. Track 3 is for insomnia.

Resting in Stillness: Integrative Restoration Psychologist Richard Miller introduces you to iRest yoga nidra and then leads two practices: a 35-minute extended relaxation practice and a 20-minute short form. Richard's soothing voice guides you through the 10-step process of iRest yoga nidra.

Yoga for Emotional Flow Psychotherapist and yogi Stephen Cope offers a prescription for emotional balance that includes breathing and visualization techniques and clear lessons in awakening the "witness consciousness."

Yoga Nidra: A Meditative Practice for Deep Relaxation and Healing with Richard Miller is an integration of book and CD audio learning. Through accessible language appropriate for every level of practice, Miller guides you through the traditional techniques of inquiry and meditation to help you realize your true nature.

Yoga Nidra II With Robin Carnes is in the nondual tradition, inspired by Richard Miller. It has a brief practice (22 minutes) and a longer practice (48 minutes), which includes a segment of chakra healing sounds that may appeal to those who are more auditory.

Practice DVDs

Below is a list of practice DVDs that I recommend. The first third and fourth, available on my Web site, I created myself.

Kripalu Dynamic Yoga, guided by renowned author, yogi, and psychotherapist Stephen Cope, offers a sequence designed to awaken the wisdom of your body as you build strength, endurance, focus, and concentration. A classical series of 30 asanas including warm-ups, standing postures, salutations, and balancing poses.

Kripalu Yoga Gentle, guided by senior Kripalu teacher Sudha Carolyn Lundeen, offers two complete and distinct yoga experiences: first flow 32 minutes, second flow 28 minutes. Includes warm-ups, a variety of floor postures, basic standing postures, a meditation-in-motion posture flow, and relaxation. Appropriate for all levels.

LifeForce Yoga to Beat the Blues: Level One includes a 75-minute practice in 12 programmable chapters so that it can be tailored to meet time constraints and individual needs. Practices are shown with modifications and contraindications, and a study guide is included. The sequence, which was shot in the mountains and valleys of Tucson, includes breathing exercises, accessible postures, mantra, and yoga nidra relaxation.

LifeForce Yoga to Beat the Blues: Level Two is for experienced practitioners who appreciate a flow of standing, supine, back-bending, and inverted postures with suggested modifications. Like Level 1, this DVD was also shot in Tucson, has 12 programmable chapters, and can be adapted to the needs of the practitioner.

Overcome Pain With Gentle Yoga Level 1 Neil Pearson guides a practice that takes the most recent scientific understanding of chronic pain and combines it seamlessly with the healing power of yoga.

Trauma Sensitive Yoga with Beth Jones includes two 30 minute sequences designed to help people living with the effects of trauma & PTSD. Breath awareness and a trauma sensitive meditation for noticing the body are offered with simple, basic postures for chair or floor.

TRAINING FOR THERAPISTS

There are training opportunities for psychotherapists who wish to include yoga-based strategies in treatment, but who may not be yoga teachers. They range from weekend programs to yoga therapy trainings that specialize in mental health and complement psychotherapy.

Breath-Body-Mind Training for Trauma

Richard P. Brown, MD, Patricia Gerbarg, MD, authors of *How to Use Herbs, Nutrients and Yoga in Mental Health Care*, and Heather Mason, MA offer a mind–body training that includes Coherent

Breathing, as described in Chapter 4, along with other breathing techniques and movement (www.haveahealthymind.com). The training includes the study of the neurophysiology behind the ways these and other mind–body strategies calm the body's central fear-processing networks and reduce the physical and psychological symptoms of anxiety, depression, and PTSD.

iRest Yoga Nidra

iRest Yoga Nidra, more fully described in Chapter 9, has been developed over the past twenty-six years by Richard Miller, PhD, a clinical psychologist, author, researcher, and yogic scholar. Two levels of five-day training are offered around the U.S. iRest has been shown to be effective in the treatment of PTSD and other mood disorders and is endorsed by the US Army Surgeon General and Defense Centers of Excellence as a complementary and alternative medicine (CAM). iRest programs are typically taught as a guided meditation. Students can expect to lie down or sit comfortably during the practice. Self-inquiry exercises similar to the description in Chapter 10 are also taught and practiced. iRest can be appropriate for a clinical setting and for at-home practice.

LifeForce Yoga Practitioner Training

My own program, LifeForce Yoga Practitioner Training, offers two levels of certification, each 58 hours of residential training, along with mentoring provided by senior LifeForce yoga practitioners who are also yoga teachers or psychotherapists. In this training, yoga and mental health professionals practice and learn to apply the yoga tools in this book, along with many other yoga-based strategies to help their clients focus, relax, have greater access to feelings within a session, and self-regulate at home. The emphasis of this training is on yoga-based techniques appropriate for a clinical setting. The faculty includes yoga and mental health professionals who are experts in the field of yoga-based treatment of depression, anxiety, and PTSD. Graduates of this program are also listed on my Web site (www.yogafordepression.com).

Mind-Body Medicine Professional Training Program

Since 1999, the Center for Mind-Body Medicine in Washington, DC, has offered certification trainings in mind-body medicine around the globe (www.cmbm.org). While not specifically a yoga program, the training includes meditation, guided imagery, biofeedback, autogenic training, breathing and movement, and self-expression through words and drawings. Founding director James S. Gordon, MD, is a pioneer in the field of using mind-body medicine to heal depression, anxiety, and psychological trauma and is the author of *Unstuck: Your Guide to the Seven-Stage Journey Out of Depression*. His faculty includes a team of physicians, psychotherapists, nurses, and somatic practitioners nationally recognized in the field of mind-body medicine.

Other Trainings for Work With Special Populations

Here are some other training opportunities, although this is not an exhaustive list.

STREET YOGA

Weekend training for those working with at-risk youth (www.streetyoga.org).

WARRIORS AT EASE

Teleseminar, residential, and mentoring. Trains yoga and meditation teachers to work in a military setting (www.warriorsatease.com).

YOGA FOR THE SPECIAL CHILD

Seven-day training for yoga teachers, educators, and health professionals to work with special needs children (www.specialyoga.com).

TRAUMA-SENSITIVE YOGA INSTRUCTION

David Emerson, who directs the yoga program at the Justice Resource Institutes Trauma Center, offers a certificate training for yoga teachers in trauma-sensitive yoga.

Phoenix Rising Yoga Therapy

Phoenix Rising Yoga Therapy (PRYT) offers an extensive certification program that involves three levels of training (currently 174 contact hours, plus 550 supervised practicum hours; www.pryt.org). PRYT practitioners learn to guide individual clients safely to the edge of deep physical sensation through hands-on support during the extended holding of a yoga posture with nonjudgmental mirroring of dialogue. In the process, there can be a release of the underlying emotions or beliefs that often manifest in chronic aches and pains. While the physical touch involved in the practice of PRYT limits its application to a setting other than the psychotherapy consultation room, many psychotherapists maintain a separate but dual practice of both psychotherapy and PRYT.

Residential Yoga & Training Centers

Esalen Institute, Big Sur, California, www.esalen.org, (888) 837-2536

Kripalu Center, Stockbridge, Massachusetts, www.kripalu.org, (866) 200-5203

Omega Institute, Rhinebeck, New York, www.eomega.org

Mount Madonna, Watsonville, California, www.mountmadonna.org

Sivananda Ashram Yoga Retreat, Paradise Island, Bahamas, www.sivananda.org/nassau, (866) 446-5934

Yogaville Satchidananda Ashram, Buckingham, Virginia, www.yogaville.org, (800) 858-9642

Yoga for the Mind

Heather Mason, MA, is the main lecturer for this training, currently offered in England. Invited guest lecturers include Daniel Siegel, MD; Robin Monro, PhD; Patricia Gerbarg, MD; and Sat Bir Khalsa, PhD. The training combines yoga mindfulness, therapeutic skills, and neuroscience in the treatment of mental health issues (email@yogaforthemind.info).

Other yoga-based workshops for mental health professionals include programs that specialize in trauma and mood disorders with leading trauma expert psychiatrist Bessel van der Kolk and psychotherapist and yoga teacher Dana Moore. Their programs are offered at Kripalu Center and elsewhere (www.traumacenter.org, www.kripalu.org).

Psychologist, yoga teacher, and author of *Yoga for Emotional Balance,* Bo Forbes, offers weekend workshops that combine restorative yoga with simple breathing in the treatment of depression and anxiety (www.elementalyoga.com).

SUGGESTED READING

Berceli, David. (2005). *Trauma-releasing exercises (TRE): A revolutionary new method for stress/trauma recovery.* BookSurge.

Brach, Tara. (2003). *Radical acceptance.* New York: Bantam Books.

Brown, Richard, Gerbarg, Patricia, & Muskin, Philip. (2008). *How to use herbs, nutrients and yoga in mental health care.* New York: Norton.

Cobb, Elissa. (2008). *The forgotten body: A way of knowing and understanding self.* Satya House Publications.

Cope, Stephen. (1999). *Yoga and the quest for the true self.* New York: Bantam.

Emerson, David & Hopper, Elizabeth. (2011) *Trauma Through Yoga: Reclaiming Your Body.* Berkeley, CA: North Atlantic Books.

Emmons, Henry. (2006). *The chemistry of joy: A three-step program for overcoming depression through Western science and Eastern wisdom.* New York: Fireside.

Forbes, Bo. (2011). *Yoga for emotional balance.* Boston: Shambhala.

Gordon, James S. (2008). *Unstuck: Your guide to the seven-stage journey out of depression.* New York: Penguin.

Hanson, Rick, & Mendius, Richard. (2009). *Buddha's brain: The practical neuroscience of happiness, love and wisdom.* Oakland, CA: New Harbinger.

Khalsa, Dharma Singh. (2001). *Meditation as medicine*. New York: Pocket Books.

Le Page, Joseph, & Le Page, Lilian. (2012). *Mudras for healing and transformation*. Shelby, NC: Integrative Yoga Therapy (www.iytyogatherapy.com).

Liebler, Nancy, & Moss, Sandra. (2009). *Healing depression the mind-body way: Creating happiness with meditation, yoga and ayurveda*. Hoboken, NJ: John Wiley and Sons.

McGonigal, Kelly. (2009). *Yoga for pain relief: Simple practices to calm your mind and heal your chronic pain*. Oakland, CA: New Harbinger.

Miller, Richard. (2006). *Yoga nidra: The meditative heart of yoga*. Boulder, CO: Sounds True.

Naiman, Rubin. (2006). *Healing night: The science of sleeping, dreaming and awakening*. Minneapolis, MN: Syren Books.

Saraswati, Satyananda. (2006). *Yoga nidra*. Munger, Bihar, India: Swami Satyananda Saraswati. (Original work published 1976)

Schwartz, Richard C. (2001). *Introduction to the internal family systems model*. Oak Park, CA: Trailheads Publications.

Shannahoff-Khalsa, David. (2006). *Kundalini yoga meditation: Techniques specific for psychiatric disorders, couples therapy and personal growth*. New York: Norton.

Shapiro, Shauna, & Carlson, Linda. (2009). *The art and science of mindfulness: Integrating mindfulness into psychology and the helping professions*. Washington, DC: American Psychological Association.

Siegel, Daniel J. (2007). *The mindful brain*. New York: Norton.

Weintraub, Amy. (2004). *Yoga for depression*. New York: Broadway Books.

Glossary

Agni Sara. "Fire washing," a practice of belly pumping; not appropriate for use in a clinical setting but can be learned from a qualified yoga teacher.

ajna. "Command," the brow point or sixth chakra.

anahata. "Unstruck sound," the heart or fourth chakra.

anuloma krama. Anuloma means "to go along with the current" or regular; krama means steps or stages. Part of a practice I call Stair Step Breathing (see Chapter 5 for directions).

asana. Literally, seat for meditation. Commonly means yoga posture.

Bhastrika. Bellows Breath (see Chapter 5 for directions).

bhavana. Cultivating, producing, or becoming, often defined as a visualized goal or image felt in body-mind.

Brahmari. "Humming bee," Bee Breath (see Chapter 4 for directions).

chakra. Wheel or vortex; often described as energy centers in the body. See *Yoga for Depression* (Weintraub, 2004) for a more thorough discussion of the chakra system and the nadis.

Chandra Bheda. Chandra means moon and bheda means division or expansion; Left Nostril Breathing. The left nostril is correlated to the right, more lunar, creative hemisphere of the brain (see Chapter 4 for directions).

Dirga Pranayama. Dirga means long and pranayama means breath control; Yogic Three-Part Breath. Creates a state of mental alertness, even as it activates the parasympathetic nervous system so that the body-mind is calm (see Chapter 4 for directions).

hara. A Japanese term for abdomen.

hatha yoga. "Physical force"; refers to the physical practice of yoga.

ida. Comfort; the nadi that runs on the left side of the body.

Kapalabhati. "Skull shining," a vigorous belly-pumping breath; not appropriate for use in a clinical setting but can be learned from a qualified yoga teacher.

karma. Action, the result of an individual's actions; cause and effect.

Kashmiri Shaivism. A nondual tradition that recognizes all life as the result of a singular divine consciousness, in this case Shiva.

Kirtan Kriya. A meditation technique from the Kundalini tradition involving mantras and mudras.

kosha model. Kosha means "sheath of our existence"; koshas are often defined as bodies, of which there are five in the yogic system: the food body (*annamaya kosha*), the energy/breath body (*pranamaya kosha*), the emotional body (*manomaya kosha*), the discerning/mental/wisdom body (*vijnanamaya kosha*), and the bliss body (*anandamaya kosha*).

kriya. Cleansing action, of which there are many kinds, including meditations and physical cleansing processes such as the use of a neti pot for nasal clearing. Here, kriya most often refers to a breathing technique that creates cleansing in the body. Most kriyas should be taught by qualified yoga teachers, are not appropriate in a clinical setting, and are contraindicated in cases of extreme anxiety, bipolar disorder with a tendency toward mania, or pregnancy.

kumbhaka. "To retain," in this case to retain the breath.

mala. Indian prayer beads, numbering 108, similar to rosary beads in appearance and function.

manipura. "Land of lustrous gems," the solar plexus or third chakra.

mantra. "Tool of the mind," sound, or tone.

mudra. "Seal," here referring to hand gestures that guide energy flow and send messages to the brain.

muladhara. "Root support," the root or first chakra, located at the perineum.

nadi. Current or pathway, a tubelike channel through the body, sometimes correlated to the nerves.

Nadi Shodhana. "Purification of the pathways," alternate-nostril breathing (see Chapter 4 for directions).

namaha. "Praise to" or, as used here, "bowing to that which is highest within."

nauli. From the root *nala*, abdominal muscles; a practice of abdominal muscle churning that is not appropriate for use in a clinical setting but can be learned from a qualified yoga teacher.

nondual. A philosophy that embraces all apparent dichotomies. Separation and the play of opposites are ultimately united in one universal consciousness. "Om mani padme om." A Buddhist prayer that means "the jewel is in the lotus."

pingala. "Tawny"; the nadi that runs on the right side of the body.

prana. Life force or life energy, here most often referred to as breath.

pranayama. Prana, life force; ayama, control. Simple yoga breath; control of life breath or life force.

pratyahara. Withdrawal or control of the senses; to focus the senses internally rather than externally.

sahasrara. "Thousand-petaled lotus"; the crown or seventh chakra.

samskaras. Activators, or karmic knots formed in reaction to our actions; the seeds of an individual's past actions.

sankalpa. Intention.

sat chit ananda. "Intelligent awareness of bliss."

shanmuki. "Six gated," referring to the six gates or openings: two eyes, two ears, nose and mouth; mudra that accompanies Bee Breath.

shanti. Peace.

Sudharshan Kriya. Breathing practice taught by the Art of Living Foundation that has been shown effective in treating depression; attending a course to learn the technique for self-care does not qualify one to teach the practice.

Surya Bheda. Surya literally means sun and bheda means division or expansion; Right Nostril Breathing. The right nostril is correlated to the left, more solar, or linear, part of the brain.

sushumna. "She who is most gracious"; the central nadi—often pictured as the spinal cord.

sutra. "Thread"; in yoga texts it refers to a stanza or an aphorism.

swadhisthana. "One's own home"; the sacral or second chakra.

"Tapas svadhyaya Ishvara-pranidhana kriya yoga." The foundational instruction given by the sage Patanjali (II, i) in the *Yoga Sutras*. It is a formula for achieving "union in action" (kriya yoga), action that is clearly aligned with one's authentic sense of self. In this sutra, Patanjali says that union in action rests on a sturdy tripod of three important elements: willful practice (tapas), self-observation (svadhyaya), and surrender (Ishvara-pranidhana). It is a prescription for optimum mental health.

Uddiyana Bandha. "Flying up lock," an energy lock; not appropriate for use in a clinical setting but can be learned from a qualified yoga teacher.

Ujjayi. "Victory"; a strong breathing practice (see Chapter 4 for directions).

vasana. "Past impression," a web of responses created by samskaras.

Viloma Krama. Viloma means "going against the current"; krama means steps or stages. Part of a practice I call Stair Step Breathing (see Chapter 5 for directions).

vishuddha. "Pure," the throat or fifth chakra.

yoga nidra. Yogic sleep.

References

Alexander, G. K., Innes, K. E., Brown, C. J., Kulbok, P., Bourguignon, C., Bovbjerg, V. E., & Taylor, A. G. (2010). "I could move mountains": Adults with or at risk for type 2 diabetes reflect on their experiences with yoga practice. *Diabetes Education, 36,* 965–975.

Badenoch, B. (2011). *The brain-savvy therapist's workbook.* New York: Norton.

Bennett, S. M., Weintraub, A., & Khalsa, S. B. (2008). Initial evaluation of the LifeForce Yoga® program as a therapeutic intervention for depression. *International Journal of Yoga Therapy, 18,* 49–57.

Berk, L. S., Tan, S. A., Fry, W. F., Napier, B. J., Lee, J. W., Hubbard, R. W., Lewis, J. E., & Eby, W. C. (1989). Neuroendocrine and stress hormone changes during mirthful laughter. *American Journal of Medical Science, 298,* 390–396.

Bernardi, L., Sleight, P., Bandinelli, G., Cencetti, S., Fattorini, L., WdowczycSzulc, J., & Lagi, A. (2001). Effect of rosary prayer and yoga mantras on autonomic cardiovascular rhythms: Comparative study. *British Medical Journal, 323,* 1446–1449.

Brown, R. P., & Gerbarg, P. L. (2009). Yoga breathing, meditation, and longevity. *Annals of the New York Academy of Sciences, 1172,* 54–62.

Calaprice, A. (2005). *The new ouotable Einstein.* Princeton, NJ: Princeton University Press.

Campbell, D. (1997). *The Mozart effect: Tapping the power of music to heal the body, strengthen the mind, and unlock the creative spirit.* New York: Avon.

Chandwani, K. D., Thornton, B., Perkins, G. H., Arun, B., Raghuram, N. V., Nagendra, H. R., Wei, Q., & Cohen, L. (2010).

Yoga improves quality of life and benefit finding in women undergoing radiotherapy for breast cancer. *Journal of the Society for Integrative Oncology, 8*(2), 43–55.

Cohen, L., Warneke, C., Fouladi, R. T., Rodriguez, M. A., & Chaoul-Reich, A. (2004). Psychological adjustment and sleep quality in a randomized trial of the effects of a Tibetan yoga intervention in patients with lymphoma. *Cancer, 100,* 2253–2260.

Ecker, B. (2010). The brain's rules for change: Translating cutting-edge neuroscience into practice. *Psychotherapy Networker, 34*(1), 43–45, 60.

Eliot, T. S. (1943). Burnt Norton. *Four quartets.* San Diego: Harcourt.

Eller, L. S. (1999). Guided imagery interventions for symptom management. *Annual Review of Nursing Research, 17*(1), 57–84.

Emoto, M., & Thayne, D. A. (2004). *The hidden messages in water.* Hillsboro, OR: Beyond Words.

Finzi, E., & Wasserman, E. (2006). Treatment of depression with botulinum toxin A: A case series. *Dermatological Surgery, 32,* 645–650.

Franzblau, S. H., Smith, M., Echevarria, S., & Van Cantford, T. E. (2006). Take a breath, break the silence: The effects of yogic breathing and testimony about battering on feelings of self-efficacy in battered women. *International Journal of Yoga Therapy, 16,* 49–57.

Frawley, D. (2010). *Mantra yoga and primal sound: Secrets of seed (bija) mantras.* Twin Lakes, WI: Lotus Press.

Gatt, J. M., Kuan, S. A., Dobson-Stone, C., Paul, R. H., Joffe, R. T., Kemp, A. H., Gordon, E., Schofield, P. R., & Williams, L. M. (2008). Association between BDNF Val66Met polymorphism and trait depression is mediated via resting EEG alpha band activity. *Biological Psychology, 79,* 275–284.

Gaynor, M. L. (2000). *The sounds of healing: A physician reveals the therapeutic power of sound, voice and music.* New York: Broadway Books.

Giedt, J. F. (1997). Guided imagery: A psychoneuroimmunological intervention in holistic nursing practice. *Journal of Holistic Nursing, 15*(2), 112–127.

Hartranft, C. (2003). *The yoga sutras of Patanjali*. Boston, MA: Shambhala.

Hately, S. (2010). Insights from working with people recovering from cancer. *International Journal of Yoga Therapy, 6*(3), 15–16.

Hölzel, B. K., Carmody, J., Evans, K. C., Hoge, E. A., Dusek, J. A., Morgan, L., Pitman, R. K., & Lazar, S. W. (2010). Stress reduction correlates with structural changes in the amygdale. *Social Cognitive and Affective Neuroscience, 5*(1), 11–17.

Innes, K. E, Selfe, T. K., & Taylor, A. G. (2008). Menopause, the metabolic syndrome, and mind-body therapies. *Menopause, 15*(5), 1005–1013.

Innes, K. E., Selfe, T. K., & Vishnu, A. (2010). Mind-body therapies for menopausal symptoms: A systematic review. *Maturitas, 66*(2), 135–149.

Innes, K. E., & Vincent, H. K. (2007). The influence of yoga-based programs on risk profiles in adults with type 2 diabetes mellitus: A systematic review. *Evidence-Based Complementary and Alternative Medicine, 4,* 469–486.

Khalsa, D. S., Amen, D., Hanks, C., Money, N., & Newberg, A. (2009). Cerebral blood flow changes during chanting meditation. *Nuclear Medicine Communications, 30,* 956–961.

Khalsa, D.S. (2001). *Meditation as medicine*. New York, NY: Pocket Books.

Kiecolt-Glaser, J. K., Christian, L., Preston, H., Houts, C. R., Malarkey, W. B., Emery, C. F., & Glaser, R. (2010). Stress, inflammation, and yoga practice. *Journal of Psychosomatic Medicine, 72,* 113–121.

Kimbrough, E., Magyari, T., Langenberg, P., Chesney, M., & Berman, B. (2010). Mindfulness intervention for child abuse survivors. *Journal of Clinical Psychology, 66,* 17–33.

Ko, H. J., & Youn, C. H. (2011). Effects of laughter therapy on depression, cognition and sleep among the community-dwelling elderly. *Geriatrics and Gerontology International, 11,* 267–274.

Lambert, K. (2008). *Lifting depression: A neuroscientist's hands-on approach to activating your brain's healing power.* New York: Basic Books..

Le Mée, K. (1994). *The origins, form, practice, and healing power of Gregorian chant.* New York: Bell Tower.

Le Page, J., & Le Page, L. (2012). *Mudras for healing and transformation.* Shelby, NC: Integrative Yoga Therapy (www.iytyogatherapy.com).

Manocha, R., Black, D., Sarris, J., & Stough, C. (2011). A randomized, controlled trial of meditation for work stress, anxiety and depressed mood in full-time workers. *Evidence-Based Complementary and Alternative Medicine,* 2011:960583. Epub 2011, June 7.

McGonigal, K. (2009). A conversation with Timothy McCall. *International Journal of Yoga Therapy, 19,* 143–147.

Miller, R. (2005). *Yoga nidra: The meditative heart of yoga.* Boulder, CO: Sounds True.

Miller, R. (2007). *Integrative restoration: Level I training manual.* Larkspur, CA: Integrative Restoration Institute.

Mora-Ripoll, R. (2010). The therapeutic value of laughter in medicine. *Alternative Therapies in Health and Medicine, 16*(6), 56–64.

Naparstek, B. (2004). *Invisible heroes: Survivors of trauma and how they heal.* New York: Bantam.

Newberg, A. B., Wintering, N., Waldman, M. R., Amen, D., Khalsa, D. S., & Alavi, A. (2010). Cerebral blood flow differences between long-term meditators and non-meditators. *Consciousness and Cognition, 19,* 899–905.

Noji, S., & Takayanagi, K. (2010). A case of laughter therapy that helped improve advanced gastric cancer. *Japan Hospitals, 29,* 59–64.

Paul, R. (2004). *The yoga of sound.* Novato, CA: New World Library.

Pease, A., & Pease, B. (2004). *The definitive book of body language.* New York: Bantam Dell.

Raghuraj, P., & Telles, S. (2008). Immedate effect of specific nostril manipulating yoga breathing practices on autonomic and respiratory variables. *Applied Psychophysiology Biofeedback, 33,* 65–75.

Rani, K., Tiwari, S., Singh, U., Agrawal, G., Ghildiyal, A., & Srivastava, N. (2011). Impact of yoga nidra on psychological general wellbeing in patients with menstrual irregularities: A randomized controlled trial. *International Journal of Yoga, 4*(1), 20–25.

Rothschild, B. (2003). *The body remembers casebook: Unifying methods and models in the treatment of trauma and PTSD.* New York: Norton.

Saper, R. B., Sherman, K. J., Cullum-Dugan, D., Davis, R. B., Phillips, R. S., & Culpepper, L. (2009). Yoga for chronic low back pain in a predominantly minority population: A pilot randomized controlled trial. *Alternative Therapies in Health and Medicine, 15*(6), 18–27.

Saraswati, S. (1998). *Yoga nidra.* Bihar, India: Yoga Publications Trust.

Schiller, D., Monfils, M. H., Raio, C. M., Johnson, D. C., LeDoux, J. E., & Phelps, E. A. (2010). Preventing the return of fear in humans using reconsolidation update mechanisms. *Nature, 463,* 49–54.

Selfe, T. K., & Innes, K. E. (2009). Mind-body therapies and osteoarthritis of the knee. *Current Rheumatology Review, 5,* 204–211.

Shahidi, M., Mojtahed, A., Modabbernia, A., Mojtahed, M., Shafiabady, A., Delavar, A., & Honari, H. (2011). Laughter yoga versus group exercise program in elderly depressed women: A randomized controlled trial. *International Journal of Geriatric Psychiatry, 26,* 322–327.

Shanker, S. S. R. (1999), The Six Distortions of Love. *Wisdom for the New Millenium.* Santa Barbara, CA: Art of Living Foundation.

Shapiro, D., Cook, I. A., Davydov, D. M., Ottaviani, C., Leutchter, A. F., & Abrams, M. (2007). Yoga as a complementary treatment of depression: Effects of traits and moods on treatment outcome. *Evidence-Based Complementary and Alternative Medicine, 4,* 493–502.

Siegel, D. (2009) speaking at the Psychotherapy Networker Symposium.

Siegel, R., & Germer, C. (2012). *Wisdom and compassion in psychotherapy: Deepening mindfulness in clinical practice.* New York: Guilford.

Streeter, C. C., Jensen, E., Perlmutter, R. M., Cabral, H. J., Tian, H., Terhune, D. B., Ciraulo, D. A., Renshaw, P. F. (2007). Yoga asana sessions increase brain GABA levels: A pilot study. *Journal of Alternative and Complementary Medicine, 13,* 419–426.

Streeter, C. C., Whitfield, T. H., Owen, L., Rein, T., Karri, S. K., Yakhkind, A., Perlmutter, R., Prescot, A., Renshaw, P. F., Ciraulo, D. A., & Jensen, J. E. (2010). Effects of yoga versus walking on mood, anxiety, and brain GABA levels: A randomized controlled MRS study. *Journal of Alternative and Complementary Medicine, 16,* 1145–1152.

Taylor, A. G., Goehler, L. E., Galper, D. I., Innes, K. E., & Bourguignon, C. (2010). Top-down and bottom-up mechanisms in mind-body medicine: Development of an integrative framework for psychophysiological research. *Explore, 6*(1), 29–41.

Telles, S., & Desiraju, T. (1991). Oxygen consumption during pranayamic type of very slow-rate breathing. *Indian Journal of Medical Research, 94,* 357–363.

Telles, S., Nagaratha, R., & Nagendra, H. R. (1994). *Breathing through a particular nostril can alter metabolism and autonomic activities.* Unpublished manuscript, Vivekananda Kendra Yoga Research Foundation.

Van der Kolk, B. A. (2006). Clinical implications of neuroscience research in PTSD. *Annals of the New York Academy of Sciences, 1071,* 277–293.

Wampold, B. E. (2001). *The great psychotherapy debate: Models, methods and findings.* Hillsdale, NJ: Lawrence Erlbaum.

Weintraub, A. (2004). *Yoga for depression: A compassionate guide to relieve suffering through yoga.* New York: Broadway Books.

Weintraub, A. (2011). *LifeForce yoga practitioner training for depression and anxiety manual*, rev. ed. Tucson: LifeForce Yoga Healing Institute.

Wood, J.V., Perunovic, E.W., & Lee, J.W. (2009, May 21) Positive self-statements for some, peril for others, *Psychological Science*, epub.

Woolger, R. J. (1988). *Other lives, other selves: A Jungian psychotherapist discovers past lives*. New York: Bantam.

Wylie, M. S. (2004a). The limits of talk. *Psychotherapy Networker, 28*, 30–45., 66- 67.

Wylie, M. S. (2004b). Mindsight: Dan Siegel offers therapists a new vision of the brain. *Psychotherapy Networker, 28* (September–October).

Index

[Page numbers in *italic* refer to illustrations.]